Sue Price

Computing for Seniors

Fifth edition

Covers Windows 8 and Office 2013

In easy steps is an imprint of In Easy Steps Limited
4 Chapel Court · 42 Holly Walk · Leamington Spa
Warwickshire · United Kingdom · CV32 4YS
www.ineasysteps.com

Fifth Edition

Notice of Liability
Every effort has been made to ensure that this book contains accurate
and current information. However, In Easy Steps Limited and the
author shall not be liable for any loss or damage suffered by readers
as a result of any information contained herein.

Trademarks
Microsoft® and Windows® are registered trademarks of Microsoft
Corporation. All other trademarks are acknowledged as belonging to
their respective companies.

In Easy Steps Limited supports The Forest Stewardship Council (FSC),
the leading international forest certification organisation. All our titles
that are printed on Greenpeace approved FSC certified paper carry the
FSC logo.

MIX
Paper from
responsible sources
FSC® C020837

Printed and bound in the United Kingdom

ISBN 978-1-84078-576-0

Contents

3 Apps from the Store   47

4 Communicate   65

5 Surfing the Web   87

6 Shopping on the Web   109

7   Letters and Reports   125

8   Money Management   145

9 Digital Photography 167

10 Presentations 181

1 Introducing Your PC

Computers aren't just for your children's work or for your grandchildren's games, they are equally meant for you. They are there to help with those must-do jobs and also with fun-to-do things. We identify and explain the hardware and software you need to do them.

The Age of the Computer

Computers today have become part of everyday life and are no longer the territory of the mathematical or technical guru. We find them in mobile phones, cars, television sets, games machines and a multitude of electronic devices, as well as the dedicated machines that we call personal computers.

Personal computers or PCs have changed dramatically over the last several years – in physical size, functionality and requirements. The progression has been from simple number crunchers, to basic office word processors and data handlers, through to today's multi-tasking and communication devices.

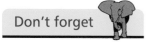
The things we now want to do with computers, and our expectations of what we can do with them, are vastly different from when the home computer first became available. We find that we need to be able to use computers and to work with the technology in today's world. It is expected that we use the Internet to check timetables, bank and utility statements and buy tickets etc. People seldom print photos of events, but share them online. We use email instead of regular postal services – it's quicker, cheaper and more efficient.

This book is designed to introduce you to the new world of computers and help you get involved. It covers the hardware available, explains technical jargon and leads you step-by-step to achieve those things that you are most likely to want to do with the computer, such as find information on the Internet, write a letter or contact friends.

By the time you have worked through the examples and suggestions in the book, you'll be completely at home with the system and ready to start your own tasks and activities.

Setting the Scene

The Operating System

This book is based on the latest version of Windows from Microsoft – Windows 8.

Windows 8 introduces the latest 'Touch' technology to personal computers that has been available for many years in places like restaurants, shops and cinemas. From punched card systems through to mouse clicks, data input has changed dramatically. The Touch technology is simpler, faster and promoted as more intuitive, than any previous interaction method.

However, all of the tasks illustrated in this book can be carried out using either the keypad or a mouse, and these alternative methods will be regularly described.

Office 2013

This is the latest version of Microsoft Office. Programs include:

- Word – for word processing tasks
- Excel – for spreadsheet, charts and data management
- PowerPoint for presentations
- Outlook – for email
- OneNote for making notes

See page 26 for full details of the Microsoft Office suite.

Windows 8 Apps

Most apps used, for example the Photos app, are already installed on your computer, along with Windows 8. Some of the other Apps illustrated, for example Games, will be downloaded from the Windows Store and installed as part of the process.

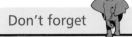

Don't forget

There are several different editions of Windows 8 for home and business use. Windows RT is a special version designed for Tablet PCs (see page 14).

The service upgrade, Windows 8.1 (from late 2013) may change the appearance, but otherwise most activities should stay the same.

Hot tip

For details of mouse buttons and pointers, see page 203.

Hot tip

There are few differences between Office 2010 and Office 2013. You will find that the activities described are usually the same in both versions.

The Desktop Computer

Although called a desktop computer, the main component which is the systems unit, is often a tower unit of varying dimensions, which can sit on top or underneath the desk. Alternative systems units may be flatter and sit on the desk underneath the screen, or even be built into the screen.

The systems unit houses all the hardware – the processor, the hard disk drive, the memory, video cards and connections for the screen and keyboard. It usually offers one or two CD or DVD drives as well as USB connections for peripheral equipment and a modem connection for broadband.

The desktop computer allows you to attach different sizes of monitor, according to your requirements and budget. The monitor and keyboard may come as part of a package with the systems unit, or can be individually selected.

Don't forget

A major advantage of the desktop model is that individual components can be replaced if they fail.

With the Windows 8 operating system, you would be advised to buy a monitor with Touch capability. Although the keyboard and mouse are still the main means of data input, Touch allows much faster navigation between the various applications and also greater ease in selecting some of the menu options. Touch-enabled monitors come with two-, five- or ten-point touch.

With a desktop computer you can attach external disk drives, multiple monitors and other peripheral hardware to extend its functions and capabilities.

Don't forget

While it is possible to attach another keyboard or monitor etc. to a laptop PC, it does remove its portability.

The Laptop Computer

Laptop PCs

With a **laptop PC** all the components will be combined into the single system, keyboard and display unit, and the mouse may be replaced by a touch pad or a pressure-sensitive toggle button. The laptop PC will usually have a CD or DVD player.

Laptop PCs are designed to be portable and therefore weight is very important. To decrease the weight, some of the features of a desktop computer may be absent.

Screen size is also an issue. If you intend to spend a lot of time browsing the Internet or working on photos, then a larger screen size would be ideal. This will, however, make the unit heavier and less portable.

Netbooks

Netbooks are even lighter and smaller in size than laptops, being on average only 1.5 inches or 4 cm thick. They do not have a CD or DVD player and will need to be connected to an external drive, by cable or wireless, for program updates. The average weight is approximately 3.5 lb or 1.5 kilo, about half of that for a laptop.

Netbooks are ideal for traveling, for checking mail, staying in touch and keeping up-to-date. However, they may prove to be tedious to use for long periods.

Battery Life

Large laptop PCs will usually only run for about two hours on the battery. The smaller netbooks may last up to 10 or more hours, depending on how many programs you are running and whether you have items such as Wi-Fi turned on. Windows 8 has new features for power management.

Hot tip

If you are thinking of buying a laptop PC, pick up the computer and check the weight to make sure it's not too heavy. You will need some kind of case for it which will also add to the weight and bulk.

13

Beware

When checking the weight of a portable PC, look to see if the weight includes the battery installed or separate.

The Tablet Computer

The Tablet PC has taken miniaturization and portability to another level. The Tablet uses Touch technology, which means that it can be used without any external means of interaction, such as an external keyboard or mouse. The keyboard is a virtual keyboard, available on the screen when required for text input.

Tablet PCs usually come with one or two cameras, forward and back facing. Most will have an orientation sensor (gyroscope) that allows you to change portrait to landscape as suitable. Some include a GPS chip to allow route maps and show information such as location and weather.

The Tablet might be supplied with a detachable keyboard, sometimes to be purchased separately. The keyboard usually acts as a protective cover, and frequently also as a stand. With a keyboard, the Tablet can be used as a Laptop computer.

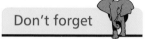

Don't forget

All these various designs of PC may run either Windows 8 or Windows RT, depending on the type of processor. Tablets based on Intel or AMD processors run Windows 8 and Tablets based on the ARM processor with its extended battery life, run Windows RT.

Manufacturers have created a variety of designs for Tablets. Lenovo, for example, offers a basic Tablet that has no keyboard, but includes a digitized pen so that you can use it just like a pen and notepad. It has an 8 MP camera and a microphone for video communication. It runs Windows 8, so gives you access to full multitasking and office functions such as presentations.

Beware

Windows RT cannot run older Windows applications and has its own version of Office 2013.

Sometimes the manufacturer incorporates a rotating mechanism so the computer can be used as a Tablet with the keyboard hidden, or as a laptop. This type of design is known as a 'Convertible', illustrated here by the Dell Convertible PC.

The Microsoft Surface

The computer used in this book for illustration and the activities described, is the Microsoft Surface. This is a Tablet computer designed and manufactured under the Microsoft label. It comes in two versions – the Surface RT and the Surface Pro.

Both machines use Touch technology and have a built-in compass and a gyroscope for adjusting orientation. There is a choice of detachable keyboards which act as a protective cover. The Touch cover is the thinner of the two with keys that register by a click 'sound', operated through the speaker. The thicker Type cover has keys that actually depress when struck.

The Surface RT, illustrated here with the Touch cover, is based on the ARM chip and has a special version of Windows. It is pre-loaded with Office 2013 Home and Student edition, a version specifically designed for it. The longer battery life of the Surface RT (up to 8 hours) and lighter weight are its advantages.

The Surface Pro is Intel-based and so is able to run the full version of Windows 8. It is supplied with a digital pen to help with precise input and is illustrated here with the Type cover. Office 2013 has to be purchased and installed separately. The Surface Pro will run older Windows programs and software from other manufacturers such as Adobe Photoshop.

The computers will have either 32GB or 64GB of memory, with the Surface Pro able to have 128GB. Both have Wi-Fi and Bluetooth technology.

Don't forget

You may need to turn the volume control up to hear the keys on the Touch cover, in a noisy environment.

Hot tip

If you intend to use the Tablet PC just for email, travel, news and entertainment, then the Surface RT would probably be sufficient for your needs. It also has the most-used Office functions in Word, Excel and Powerpoint.

Connections

All types of computers come with facilities that will allow you to connect other hardware. There are three main types of connections:

- **Device-specific**, such as for the monitor or network
- **Generic USB connections**, used for multiple device types (see below)
- **Wireless (radio) connections**, e.g. for broadband or printer

The picture below illustrates the connection points on the back of a standard laptop computer. There are more connection points on the sides.

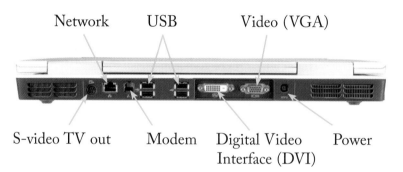

Network   USB   Video (VGA)

S-video TV out   Modem   Digital Video   Power
Interface (DVI)

USB Ports

These connection points are used by a multiplicity of devices including cameras, flash drives (memory sticks), external disk drives, projectors, navigation systems and iPods.

Wireless Connections

The laptop illustrated above has a built-in wireless transmitter/receiver, evidenced only by an indicator light on the keyboard when the machine is operating. Wireless, or Wi-Fi broadcasting is used for larger items such as broadband routers, Internet connections and printers.

Bluetooth wireless (see page 18) is used for smaller equipment such as mobile phones and PDAs.

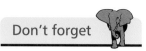

Don't forget

Desktop and laptop computers will come with several USB and other connection points. These are minimal on Tablet PCs. Network and Internet access is achieved through Wi-Fi.

Hot tip

Using wireless connections means few or no trailing cables. It allows for greater flexibility when positioning equipment. Wi-Fi broadband also has the great advantage of allowing visitors to share your Internet connection.

Computer Peripherals

Printer

There are two main types of printers – the laser printer, which uses toner cartridges (like a photocopier) and the inkjet printer, which uses ink cartridges.

Laser printers are ideal for higher volumes of printing. They may be monochrome (with black toner only) or color and produce excellent results for text, but they are not generally suitable for printing photographs.

If you choose an inkjet printer, make sure to select one that has a separate black ink cartridge. For the colored inks, there may be a single tricolor cartridge, which is suitable for occasional color printing.

For serious color printing, such as digital photographs, it is better to choose a printer with individual color cartridges. This allows you to change just the one cartridge when a single color gets depleted – a much more economical proposition. Many mid-priced ink-jet printers come with a feature such as PictBridge which allows you to print directly from your digital camera memory card.

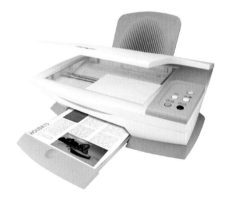

You could consider a dedicated photo printer. These are easy to use and come with photo-sized paper. However, many are limited to 6" x 4" prints, with a few offering 7" x 5".

Scanner

This allows you to copy letters, documents and pictures, so you can store their images on your hard disk. The scanner can also be used in conjunction with your printer, to give you photocopier capabilities. You can buy combined printer and scanner units, which are known as all-in-one printers, as pictured above.

Beware

Some inkjet printers use a mixture of colored inks to produce a rather muddy greenish-black.

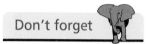

Don't forget

Many printers come with wireless capability.

Hot tip

The card reader on a printer can usually handle several different types of data card, but make sure that the type used by your camera is supported.

...cont'd

Digital Camera

You can transfer the pictures from your digital camera to your PC. From there, you can use editing software to enhance or make corrections. You can upload them to the Internet to share with friends, or copy them to DVD to play back on your TV.

You may be able to connect your digital camera directly to your PC, or you may have a card reader that allows you to take the storage card from your digital camera and read the contents on your PC. Both methods involve using a USB connection.

Hot tip

When one Bluetooth-enabled device comes within the range of another similarly equipped, they will try to automatically connect.

Some cameras have Bluetooth capability. If your printer was similarly equipped, you would be able to transfer images for printing without any cable connection.

Flash Drive

This is also referred to as a memory stick, pen drive or external drive and is attached through the USB port. Its purpose is to enable you to transfer or store data – pictures, films, music or just document files. A 1 GB drive will hold up to 540 standard-size photos, 12 hours of MP3 music files, or 6 hours of video files. They can be up to 256 GB capacity.

iPod or MP3 Player

At the base level, these systems simply play music and sometimes radio. They use the computer to manage, store and provide backup of the music files. The more sophisticated of these systems take photos, provide satellite navigation, access to email and the Internet and also act as a mobile phone.

Don't forget

Blackberry and Windows Phone are examples of Smart phones. A PDA such as the HP iPaq is a Personal Digital Assistant.

Smart Phone or PDA

You can synchronize and manage the emails, contacts and calendar information on these devices using Windows 8.

Technical Jargon Explained

Wi-Fi

Wi-Fi is used to create a wireless network, allowing you to connect a number of computers and devices and share access to the Internet, without having to string cables. Wi-Fi is enabled through the broadband or ADSL connection and router which sends a radio signal to the computers. Wi-Fi is also found in public places such as airports and coffee shops.

Bluetooth

Bluetooth is a way of exchanging data wirelessly over short distances, and does away with any need for wiring. It uses a special radio frequency to transmit data and is very secure. It allows high-speed communication between PCs and other computing devices including mobile phones. You can use a Dongle if required, plugged into your computer, to connect via Bluetooth.

The SIM Card

SIM cards are used in mobile phones, and are network specific, but can also be used in Tablet and laptop computers. You would then use your phone network to connect to the Internet or for email. This can prove to be an expensive option, especially if traveling abroad.

Screen Resolution

The screen resolution is measured in picture elements or pixels. To use the full Windows 8 functions, including SnapApps (see page 43) you need 1366 by 768 pixels as the minimum. To run an individual Windows 8 app, you need a minimum of 1024 by 768 pixels.

Touch

Touch-enabled monitors are not just for Tablet PCs, they may be added to a desktop computer. They can be two-point, five-point or 10-point. The minimum required for Windows 8 is five point touch. This supports the full range of touch gestures including stretching, pinching and swiping.

Capacitive or inductive pens are often included to enable more precision when using touch operations.

Don't forget

You can also connect PCs and devices, and share your Internet connection, using Ethernet adapters and network cables.

Hot tip

Bluetooth is particularly convenient for transferring files from one mobile phone to another or sending music and photos between a PC and a mobile phone.

The Operating System

Just as important as the equipment that makes up your PC, are the items of software that have been included with it. The primary element is the **operating system**, to provide the working environment. This will normally be Microsoft Windows.

The Windows operating system runs all the hardware and software on your PC. It allows you to access programs, save files to internal and external hard drives, and personalize and change computer settings to your own requirements. It enables you to communicate with the printer and other peripheral devices.

Don't forget

There are several versions of Windows, including Windows Vista and Windows XP, but in this book, we will assume for illustration purposes that you have Windows 8 installed.

The image above shows the Windows Start screen, with tiles for the programs installed. Several tiles will change automatically to display updated information. The image shown below is of the Windows Desktop, with a layout more familiar to users of previous versions of Windows.

Hot tip

The Windows Desktop is accessed from the tile at the bottom left of the Start screen.

Windows 8 Editions

There are four editions of Windows 8. The Base edition contains the main features including touch capability, Internet Explorer 10, Windows 8 apps and Windows Store.

Windows 8 Pro is for more advanced users and technical professionals. The Enterprise edition is purely for business and is not supplied as a retail pack.

Features	Base	Pro / Enterprise	RT
Processor support	x32/64	x32/64	x32
Multi-touch capability	Yes	Yes	Yes
Support for Desktop programs	Yes	Yes	Restricted
Upgradable from Windows 7	Yes	Yes	No
Home Group	Create/join	Create/join	Join only
Windows Media Player	Yes	Yes	No
Windows Media Center	No	Available as an add-in	No
File History	Yes	Yes	Yes
Microsoft Office	No	No	Yes

Windows RT is only available pre-installed on Tablets with the ARM processor. It does not support conventional Windows programs, though more significantly, it does include a version of Microsoft Office 2013 designed specifically for it.

Don't forget

The Intel and AMD processors used for Windows 8 PCs operate in both 32 bit and 64 bit modes. There are versions of Windows 8 and Office 2013 for each mode. For most users, there's no significant difference between the modes, although 64 bit is preferred if you are going to be working with really large Excel spreadsheets.

Hot tip

The ARM processor of Windows RT is a Reduced Instruction Set Computer (RISC) processor with enhanced power-saving features used for mobile phones and media players.

Windows 8 Apps

In addition to the operational software, you'll find that various applications (apps) are included with Windows 8 and will be displayed as a series of tiles when you start.

Mail

When you start your computer and sign in to your account you will automatically get the associated email account set up. The Mail App shows a count of arriving email and gives direct access to the account.

People

Your contacts will be displayed here, together with quick links to the most popular social networking sites, such as Facebook or Twitter. Contacts can be synchronised between your PC and phone.

Calendar

This app displays your planned activities on a daily, weekly or monthly basis. It can be synced with your phone or permitted contacts.

Messaging

Use this app to chat with friends and contacts. Interaction is effectively live and by means of the keyboard, rather than face-to-face, and can also be through Facebook.

Photos

Once you begin to take or upload photos to your PC, they will be displayed with the Photos app. Photos can be obtained from another computer, mobile phone or from online sources such as Flickr.

Weather

This shows the current weather situation in various cities throughout the world, but can be customized to show the weather in your chosen location.

Camera

The Tablet has built-in lenses, forward and back facing, to allow photography or video messaging, and includes a built-in microphone. You can specify the resolution and aspect ratio.

Other Installed Apps

- **News** – provided by Bing (Microsoft's search engine)
- **Internet Explorer** – for surfing the Web
- **Maps** – will show your current position, show an aerial or road view and let you search for directions
- **Games** – none are initially installed; this is a link to the Windows Store to get started
- **Music** – a link to the Windows Store. Again, no music is installed but you can visit the Windows Store or copy music from another source
- **Sports** – news reports from newspapers, sports channels and links to follow favorite teams, provided by Bing
- **Travel** – photographs and information about worldwide destinations, including local weather conditions and currency exchange rates
- **Financial news** – including current stock market prices, articles and stock trading prices

Hot tip

The Office 2013 applications can be accessed through both the Metro interface and the Desktop interface.

23

The Desktop App

This app gives you access to the Desktop interface, where, if you have used a previous version of Windows, you will find familiar features and layout.

The Desktop interface is where you can install and run software from other companies or older applications.

Don't forget

If you are running Windows RT, you will be unable to run older applications.

Desktop Apps

The Desktop, accessed through the Desktop icon, has a series of its own applications. These are inherited from previous versions of Windows, and provide a number of useful and necessary functions.

File Explorer

This program, with a shortcut icon on the taskbar, lets you view the contents of your disk drives. You can use it to navigate the drives and folders and to organize and view your files.

Internet Explorer

Windows 8 comes with Internet Explorer 10. Use it to browse and surf the World Wide Web. You can choose your own Home page, create favorite sites and use it to travel and shop from the comfort of your home.

Ease of Access

Programs in the Ease of Access category include Magnifier, Narrator and Speech Recognition, all utilities to customize your computer for personal requirements.

Control Panel

This gives you access to system and security settings, lets you create or join a network, manage hardware and other devices, uninstall a program and adjust screen resolution. Here, you can set up Family Safety and create accounts for family members, personalize your system and change the language, region and clock settings.

Notepad

Text files created with Notepad are plain text documents, with no formatting. These files are generic and can be read by almost any application.

Calculator

Calculator has advanced functions as well as standard mathematical calculations. It offers Scientific, Programmer and Statistic functions along with Date calculation and Unit conversion.

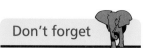
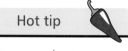

Windows 8 Only Apps

The apps described on the previous pages will operate in either Windows 8 or Windows RT. The following apps and programs are Windows 8 only and will not run on Windows RT. They include:

WordPad

This is a word processor with limited function, but would fulfill most

word processing requirements. It has the usual features of document layout, text justification, find/replace and can handle inserted pictures.

Windows Media Player

This program handles your computer's libraries of music, video, pictures and other recorded material, enabling you to

play or view the media. With it, you can manage media files, create playlists or add tags of date, genre, etc. to files.

Programs from Other Suppliers

Adobe Photoshop is a popular program, offering full image management. It handles all image types and allows simple photo editing (cropping, red-eye reduction, air-brushing, etc.), as well as more complex activities used by professional photo studios.

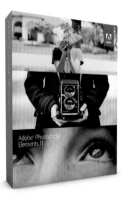

Other image management programs that require Windows 8 are Paintshop Pro and Irfanview, both free to download from the Internet.

Programs from independent software writers, such as music programs/editors, games – Chess, Bridge, etc. will also require the full version of Window 8. This category would also include software for peripherals, such as that specifically written for cameras and other devices.

Don't forget

More Windows 8-only apps can be found in the Windows Store (see page 48).

Hot tip

Most programs written for Windows 7 will run under Windows 8. To check a particular program, go to the Microsoft website at www.microsoft.com and search for the Windows Compatibility Center, where you will find a list of compatible programs.

Microsoft Office

Microsoft Office is an integrated suite of applications. Office 2013 comes in several editions, each edition offering a different combination of programs. Below is a table showing the programs included in the various versions.

Hot tip

The Surface RT Tablet computer comes with Office 2013 already installed. For other computers, it has to be bought and installed separately.

Hot tip

In integrated applications, the individual programs work together.
So, for example, a table created in the spreadsheet can be copied and pasted into the word processor.

Programs	Home and Student	Home and Business	Standard	Professional	Professional Plus
Word	Yes	Yes	Yes	Yes	Yes
Excel	Yes	Yes	Yes	Yes	Yes
PowerPoint	Yes	Yes	Yes	Yes	Yes
OneNote	Yes	Yes	Yes	Yes	Yes
Outlook	No	Yes	Yes	Yes	Yes
Publisher	No	No	Yes	Yes	Yes
Access	No	No	No	Yes	Yes
InfoPath	No	No	No	No	Yes
Lync	No	No	No	No	Yes

The version of Office 2013 that comes with the Surface RT is the Home and Student edition, which has been specially written to work with the ARM processor. Functionally, it offers the same features.

Start Your PC

When you start Windows 8 for the very first time, you will have the opportunity to choose a number of settings that will apply to your new computer.

1 Switch on the computer. The first step is to choose one of the 25 color schemes offered or you could just accept the default Blue scheme if preferred

27

Hot tip

These same steps are required if you are upgrading from Windows 7.

2 Provide a name for your computer. This name will be used to identify your computer, if at some point later, you connect to a home network. Click Next

Don't forget

You will be able to customize your settings at any time, once you have decided which changes you would like.

3 Select Use Express Settings. These settings are for security and other personalization. They include Windows Firewall, Windows Defender and Windows Update

4 At this point, Windows 8 will turn on sharing and search for any local network

Microsoft Account

When you have applied the settings, you will now need to supply an email address to sign in to Windows 8.

If you already have an email account you can use that, but the preferred option is to create or use a Microsoft account. Microsoft make it easy by offering a choice on the initial Sign in screen.

1 Supply your Microsoft email address if you have one and click or tap Next. All you need to do then is supply the password and you will be presented with the Start screen

2 To create a Microsoft account select Sign up for a new email address. You'll be prompted to suggest a name and offered options if it is already in use. You also will need to supply a password

3 You could use a different email such as Gmail. You would then need to supply some personal details to have the email address associated with a Microsoft account

4 If you'd prefer at this point not to supply any email address you could just create a simple sign in and password for security purposes. You could then create a Microsoft account later

2 Learn and Discover

In this chapter you will discover how to find, open and close programs, get some practice with the touch and mouse operations and at the same time enjoy some simple apps.

Getting Started

When you start your computer in Windows 8 you will initially see the Windows logo, with a spinning circle of dots to show the operating system is loading. This is followed by the Lock screen as shown below.

Hot tip

Security on the Internet is explained on page 104.

Hot tip

The full range of Touch gestures is illustrated on page 32.

2:47
Thursday, March 21

Hot tip

The arrow to the left of the account picture indicates that there is more than one user account defined on this computer.

1 Swipe up, click the mouse button (see page 33) or press a key to reveal the Sign in window. The window offers the opportunity to start the Ease of Access functions, described on page 206. It also displays the Shut down button

Hot tip

If you're not sure if you have typed the password correctly, click the eye to the right of the password, to reveal the underlying text.

Sue Price
sue.j.price@live.com

2 Type your Microsoft account password, then press the enter key or tap or mouse click the arrow

3 The Welcome message is displayed whilst the account settings are applied to your computer

4 The Start screen is then presented with tiles for each program currently installed

Desktop App   Windows 8 Apps   Live Tiles   App Group

5 Swipe from right to left to reveal more tiles and those for Microsoft Office if it is installed

Hot tip

The tiles may differ from those shown here if your supplier has made any changes to the original setup.

Hot tip

To the right is your username which you can customize with your own photograph or account picture.

31

Don't forget

Microsoft Office will be automatically installed on the Surface RT. For other computers it must be purchased separately, but can be installed by your supplier.

Touch Gestures

With a Tablet PC, or a monitor with Touch capability, you can use Windows 8 Touch to open and use the programs as shown below:

 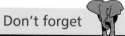
When asked to		What you do	What happens
Tap		Tap once on an item	Opens the tile or object
Press and hold		Press and hold your finger down for a few seconds	Shows related menu options, right mouse click equivalent
Slide		Drag your finger across the screen	Scrolls through what's on the screen
Pinch		Pinch thumb and forefinger together	Zooms out (makes the image smaller)
Stretch		Move thumb and forefinger apart	Zooms in (magnifies the image)
Rotate		Put two or more fingers on an item and turn your hand	Rotates that item
Slide item a short distance		Tap and slide an item a short amount down	Selects that item
Slide to rearrange		Tap and drag an item to a new location	Moves that item

Swipe Actions

Swiping from the edge of the screen reveals differing options, depending on the edge chosen:

Edge Selected	Action
From right edge	Opens the Charms bar
From left edge	Reveals the App Switcher Snaps apps side by side
From top edge	Show commands on App bar
From bottom edge	Show commands on App bar
Swipe and drag from the top to the bottom edge	Closes the app

Using the Mouse or Touch pad

You can use the mouse or touch pad to achieve the same functions, by using the left and right mouse buttons, the top edge and the four Hot Spots on the Windows 8 screen:

Action	Effect
Left mouse click	Selects and opens the item
Right mouse click	Selects the item and reveals the Apps command bar
Click the top left Hot Spot	Reveals the last used app
Click the top left Hot Spot and drag down	Reveals the App Switcher
Click the bottom left Hot Spot	Reveals the Start screen or last used app
Click the top right Hot Spot and drag down	Reveals the Charms bar
Drag down, with mouse 'hand' from top to very bottom	Closes the app or program
Drag bottom scroll bar or move the mouse to each edge	Moves screen sideways

Hot tip

The Hot Spots are in the very corners of the screen and can only be used with a mouse.

Hot tip

Scroll bars appear at the bottom and/ or side of the screen when you move the mouse arrow.

Hot tip

The left and right mouse buttons can be swapped for left-handed people. See page 203.

33

Keyboard Shortcuts

The Windows Logo key (WinKey), either on the keypad or on the monitor of a tablet pc, acts as a toggle, switching between the Start screen and the previously-active app.

You can use the WinKey and other keys in combination to perform the same actions as those achieved with gestures or the mouse. There is an action for almost all alphabet keys. The following are the most useful:

Don't forget

It's not essential to learn or use these keyboard shortcuts, but you will find them useful on occasion.

WinKey + C	Display Charms bar
WinKey + F	Open Search charm for Files
WinKey + I	Open the Settings charm
WinKey + L	Lock your PC or switch users
WinKey + O	Lock the screen orientation
WinKey + Q	Open Search charm for Apps
WinKey + U	Open Ease of Access Center
WinKey + W	Open Search charm for Settings
WinKey + Z	Show commands available in app

There are also a number of keyboard shortcuts that can be used, but are most useful within the Office products.

Ctrl + X	Cut
Ctrl + C	Copy
Ctrl + V	Paste
Ctrl + Z	Undo the last action (except Save)
Ctrl + Y	Redo
Ctrl + S	Save the document
Ctrl + P	Print

Discover the Apps

Swiping or moving the Start screen sideways reveals more available apps. However, there are many more apps already installed on the PC. To view the full list:

 From the Start screen swipe up, or right mouse click on a blank area, to reveal the App bar

Tap or click the All Apps button displayed to view the complete list, including those which use the Desktop environment

Don't forget

The Microsoft Office programs, and many others shown here, run from the Desktop. They can be started from here or from the Desktop icon.

Tap the Windows key to return to the Start screen

Open Some Apps

The Weather App

The tile on the Start screen indicates the current weather situation in your local area.

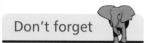
1 Tap the tile to open the program and you will see the five day forecast, with the hourly forecast displayed to the right

2 Swipe left to see further details, such as national and regional weather maps. Historical data and averages are also shown

3 Swipe up or down from an edge to display the options and the settings

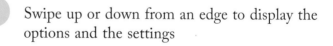

The Finance App

Brought to you by Bing Finance, this app displays financial news for your location, including newspaper reports, money saving tips and a regular update of the stock market.

1   Swipe sideways and select an article to read further details. Tap the Back arrow to return to the main Finance information

2   Also included is a Watchlist of current stocks and shares and a list of Market Movers. Tap the Add button to add your choice of shares to the Watch list

3   Swipe down or right mouse click to reveal the menu. Select Currencies for major exchange rates. Tap the Converter for your own calculation

The SkyDrive App

The Windows 8 SkyDrive app is a program that allows you to backup files or store files in the 'Cloud'. Using the Cloud means that you can store files securely, and access them where and when you want them, as long as you have an Internet connection.

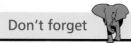
When you created your Microsoft account, you will have been granted some SkyDrive storage automatically. To view the SkyDrive:

1. Open the SkyDrive tile to see the standard SkyDrive folders

2. Each folder shows how many files it contains. Tap or click to open the folder and view the contents

3. Each file indicates the program used to create it, for example, W for Word

4. Select an individual file and it opens in the associated software. With a Word document, it opens on the Desktop on your computer

Upload to SkyDrive

1 Tap or click to open the SkyDrive app and then open the folder in which you wish to place the file. At this point you are looking at the folders in the 'Cloud', as shown on the previous page

shown on the previous page

 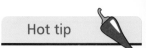
2 Swipe up to display the App bar and Select Upload

3 Navigate through the folders on your computer, using Go up, or click the arrow next to Files for direct access to other folders

4 Locate and select the file and then click or tap the Add to SkyDrive button. Selected files are listed at the bottom of the screen

5 The upload speed depends on the size of the files and your broadband connection

Search for an App

Windows 8 comes with up to twenty apps already installed. It also has a number of Windows accessories, which provide extra functions, such as Calculator or Notepad. Not all these apps are displayed on the Start screen. To find a specific program or app:

1 Swipe up or right mouse click to display the Apps bar. Then tap the All apps button. The full list will be shown for you to select

2 Alternatively, swipe from the right edge, or mouse click the Hot Spot in the right corner of the screen to reveal the Charms bar with its functions

3 Click or tap Search and start to type the name of the app you want. By default, Search will search the Apps category

4 Search displays apps that match the name, eliminating apps as you type

5 Search will also find features in Settings and Files that match the criteria – in this case options or files that start with the letter 'C'

Desktop Apps

Calculator

Calculator is a typical Desktop program in that it runs in a window, rather than full screen, like the new Weather or Finance app shown previously. It is, however, atypical in that its window cannot be resized in the way that the window for other Desktop programs such as Word or Excel can.

Hot tip

Calculator is an example of a program that runs in the Desktop environment.

1. Select Calculator and you will see it open on a different background. This is the Desktop interface which is where the original Windows programs and accessories are designed to operate

2. Calculator uses the Menu bar to access functions. Click View to see the drop-down list of different styles of calculator

Hot tip

When you open any application, you will see its icon on the Taskbar at the bottom of the desktop.

3. Click, for example, Unit conversion. You can then select from a full range of units and convert in either direction

4. Numbers can be entered using the numeric keypad (if available), the number keys or by using the mouse to select

App Switcher View

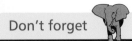
You can switch between open apps by pressing the Windows key, which will take you back to the previously-viewed app. With several apps open Windows 8 gives you other ways of switching directly to the required app.

1 With a touchscreen, from any app or from the Start screen itself, drag to the right from the left edge and release. You will see all open apps displayed. Tap to select the one required

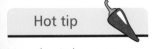

2 With the mouse, slide down the left screen edge to reveal the App Switcher. Click on the app to open

3 Press WinKey + Tab. This displays the App Switcher panel. As you press the Tab key the focus moves down the apps

4 Press Alt + Tab for the open apps to be displayed across the middle of the monitor. Tap and release the Tab key when you are on the one you want

View Side-by-Side

Windows 8 has a feature called Snap. This allows two apps to share the screen and to be viewed simultaneously. To enable this you must have a high resolution monitor – the minimum is 1366 by 768 pixels.

1 Just drag from the left edge to cycle through the open apps. Drag slowly and release to display two apps together

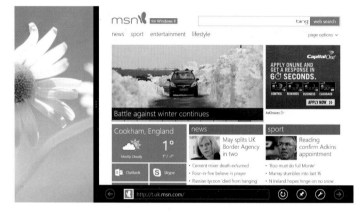

2 The separating bar can be dragged across the screen to change the priority, but has only two positions – partially left or right

3 With the App Switcher displayed, select a thumbnail and drag partly to the right (too far and the second app will take over the full screen)

4 Alternatively, right click a thumbnail and choose Snap left or Snap right

5 Each app works independently. When you switch from app to app, Windows 8 enables the new app to take over and the previous app to run in the background (if supported)

Close the Apps

There are two types of programs that run in Windows 8. The apps designed specifically for the new Windows 8 interface, and the programs developed over the years that run on the traditional Desktop.

The new apps run full screen and have no obvious way of closing. In most cases they don't need to be closed if you close your computer. Any changes made to settings are done while using the program and there is generally no additional data that needs to be saved. However, if you wish to close an app there are several ways including:

1. With a touch screen, drag from the very top to off the bottom. The app will shrink as it is dragged down the screen and close as it disappears

2. With the mouse, take the arrow to the top of the screen where it will change to a hand, and drag down and off the bottom

3. Use the App Switcher as illustrated on the previous page. Right mouse click and select Close

The Desktop App

These programs run in a window with a title bar at the top. The title bar has Minimize, Maximize and Close buttons. When you want to close a program, first save any data, text etc. and then click Close.

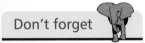
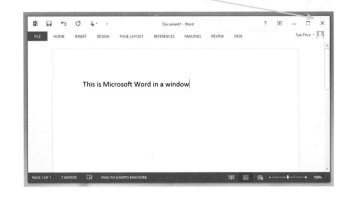

Close the Computer

During your working time, it is perfectly acceptable to just leave the computer and let it go into "Sleep" mode if you will be returning to use it fairly soon. When you wish to start using it again you simply need to enter the password. The computer has remained signed on to the Windows account.

To perform a complete shut down when the need arises you can use the following method:

1   Reveal the Charms bar, swiping from the right or using the right-hand Hot Spot, and click Settings

2   Tap the Power options and choose Shut down to close the computer completely

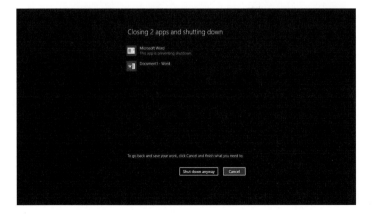

3   If there are any Desktop apps open, it will warn you and give you the opportunity to Cancel and return to the app

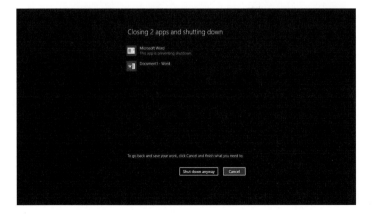

4   If you choose to shut down anyway, you could lose any unsaved data

5   Without any open apps, Windows 8 will just close

Hot tip

With more than one user defined on the PC, when you switch user you have the opportunity to shut down.

45

Don't forget

The Start screen doesn't show which apps are open, only the Desktop has a Taskbar which indicates open programs.

...cont'd

Don't forget

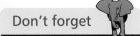

When Windows 8 needs to apply updates, you will be warned not to turn the computer off (see page 224).

Hot tip

On a keyboard with Function keys, press Alt + F4. This key combination will close the active Desktop app, then shut down Windows 8 itself.

Restart Your Computer

You will need to restart your computer for apps and programs to apply updates. Programs from independent suppliers, such as virus protection, will download updates but warn you that you will need to restart for them to be applied.

Selecting Restart closes the computer. It restarts automatically and you will need to enter your password. Any apps or programs that were previously open will need to be re-opened.

Ctrl + Alt + Del

This key combination is usually a last resort when the system or program has completely frozen and nothing is working. It takes you to the Lock screen.

1. Select Task Manager on the Lock screen to display all open applications. It will indicate which program is not responding. You can then choose to close just that program

2. Alternatively, tap or click the Shut down button and choose Shut down to turn the computer off altogether

3. You may need to press and hold the power switch on the computer itself if nothing else works

3 Apps from the Store

This chapter covers how to navigate the Windows Store, and find and download some of the apps that will enhance the functions of your computer or Tablet PC. You will be able to read books, select and play music or games with the chosen apps.

The Windows Store

The Windows Store is the only means of distributing Windows 8 apps to users. The apps may be free or chargeable, but are supplied through the Store so they can be checked by Microsoft for security and malware issues.

As we saw in Chapter One, you need to create an account to start Windows 8. The recommended account is at Live.com (or Outlook.com). With this account you have immediate access to the Windows Store. To visit the Store:

Don't forget

Windows 8 comes with some new apps and some original Windows applications. You will need to visit the Store to get some of those that were previously included.

Don't forget

When you visit the Windows Store, you will only be offered apps that will run on your particular system. So if, for example, you have a Surface RT computer, you will only see suitable apps.

1 Select the Windows Store tile. It opens on the Spotlight selection, displaying apps from several categories which are recommended to get you started

2 Select, for example, Top free. Swipe or scroll sideways to see the full range of apps in this category. Each tile indicates the category and Users' star rating

3 To return to the main Store, press the back arrow

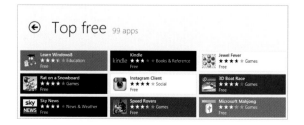

Explore the Store

The Store divides its offerings into categories to help you search through the thousands of available products. Each category subdivides into Top paid, Top free and New releases. To navigate the Store:

1. Swipe left or right or use the scroll bar at the bottom of the screen which appears when you move the mouse arrow

2. Click or tap a category title such as Books and Reference to open the category and access the search filters

3. Click the down arrow on each filter to refine the selection

4. The search is dynamic, eliminating unsuitable apps as the filters are applied. A count is given of the number that meet the criteria

5. Use the Sort by field to arrange the selection

6. Click the Back arrow to return to the main Store

49

Hot tip

There is a huge range of apps available in the Windows Store. Categories include:

Games
Social
Entertainment
Photo
Music and Video
Books and Reference
Lifestyle
Finance
Shopping
Productivity
Tools
Security
Education
Government

Don't forget

The Surface Picks section is specifically selected to help you get the most out of a Surface tablet computer. The apps may be chargeable or free and cover a wide range of activities.

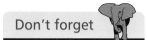

Search for a Specific App

If an app has been particularly recommended to you, the quickest way to locate it is to use the Search facility:

1 With the Windows Store open, drag from the right edge of the screen, or click the Hotspot in the top right of the screen to reveal the Charms bar

2 Click or tap the Search function, then type in the name of the particular app. As you type, matching items will appear under the Search field. Select or ignore the suggestions as appropriate

Windows Store Options

When you swipe down or right click the Windows Store screen, you have only two functions:

- **Home** – selecting Home takes you straight back to the main Windows Store screen

- **Your apps** – the Windows Store (itself an app) keeps a record of all the apps on your computer. This provides a quick way to make sure that apps that you find useful on one computer can be quickly and easily installed on another, without searching for each individually

Your Store Account

As described previously, you need a registered Microsoft account to use Windows 8 fully. This account provides access to the Windows Store and lets you download free apps. However, if you wish to buy an app you must supply credit card details. To supply these details and set other preferences:

1 With the Windows Store open, display the Charms bar, and click or tap Settings

2 Select Your account from the list of options

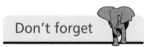

> ← **Your account**
>
> sue.j.price@live.com
> Sign in with a different account
> **Change user**
>
> **Payment and billing info**
> Before you can purchase an application, you need to add a payment method to your account.
>
> **Add payment method**
>
> Always ask for your password when buying an application
> Yes

3 Select Add payment method and follow the on-screen prompts to supply credit card details

4 Make sure that the option to always ask for your password when buying is set to Yes

5 You will also see a list of computers registered on the account (in this instance there is only one, the Surface). If you no longer use a particular computer you can Remove it from the list

> **Your PCs**
>
> When you install an app on a PC from the Windows Store, the name of that PC will appear here. You can install the apps you get from the Store on 5 PCs.
>
> SURFACE
>
> **Remove**

Don't forget

The account with Microsoft is free. You only need to supply a credit card if you wish to purchase an app.

Don't forget

Even free apps, once downloaded, are registered as purchased.

Hot tip

Have a look at the other Settings within the Windows Store, but remember that they are usually set for best performance and do not need to be changed.

Download Apps

The Kindle App

This is an example of the kind of app available through the Store for free. It is a text reader that handles the 'Kindle' format and gives you access to over a million books, including best sellers and the latest releases. Particularly suited to tablet computers and small hand-held devices, this app can synchronize your reading across devices, it lets you customize the font size for easy reading and means you can take lots of books away with you on holiday, without needing a second suitcase.

Don't forget

Notice the reminder in the top right hand corner that Updates are available for several apps. You tap this message to list the updates (see page 64).

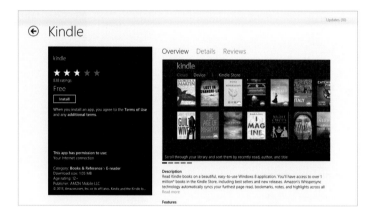

Don't forget

Free books from sites such as Project Gutenberg cannot be read by the Windows 8 Kindle app. However you can use other readers as described on page 55.

1. Click or tap the Install button. The app is downloaded and you are informed that the app has been installed

2. Return to the Start screen, by pressing the Windows button or using the App Switcher

3. The new Kindle app tile will appear, added to the far right of the existing tiles

4. To use the Kindle app you will need to sign in with or create an Amazon account

5 Click Create account and follow the on-screen instructions, supplying name, email address and password

6 The website opens displaying Kindle eBooks for sale. Use the Search field to locate a specific title, or browse by category

7 To navigate the website, swipe up or down, or right mouse click to reveal the navigation options and the open windows

8 Select Your Account to view Your Orders, manage your payments or change your account settings

...cont'd

Purchase a Book

 Search for "free Kindle books" and click to select the Kindle edition of the volume

 Click the down arrow under Deliver to: to view potential devices

3 Choose the device, in this case Sue's Kindle for Windows 8, and click Buy now with 1-Click

4 With a free book, no charge is involved. The book is downloaded and appears on your Surface or Windows 8 computer

5 If you already have an Amazon account with a credit card defined, 1-Click will automatically charge your card when a chargeable book is downloaded

6 Open the Kindle app and select the book. Tap the left or right of the screen to page through the book. Swipe up or right mouse click to open the options

7 Choose, for example, Pin to Start to enable easy access to the book. A new tile appears to the right of the Start screen

8 The Kindle app will remember your reading point and the book can be synced across devices

Other Readers

Books come in a variety of formats, and not all apps handle all formats. So it's useful to be aware of other readers and the formats they handle. If, for example, you were to visit the Gutenberg site for free online books, you would see that they can be downloaded in several formats.

Don't forget

The Windows 8 Kindle app only works with books downloaded from the Amazon website.

Book Bazaar Reader

For books in EPUB, MOBI, FB2 and TXT formats, this app gives you access to free books from many sources. It offers the usual reader functions such as adding bookmarks and notes, changing the font size and page orientation and night reading mode. It also has a library function that enables you to manage your book collection.

Reader

This app comes as a standard program on Windows 8, but is only listed on the All apps screen. Reader handles PDF and XPS files. When you are browsing the Internet and open a PDF document, it uses Reader for its display. Reader has a limited set of functions, but does allow for screen rotation, and to search within the document. See page 100 for more detail.

Hot tip

You could add Reader as a tile on the Start screen, but it is generally invoked automatically by opening an online document.

Free Books

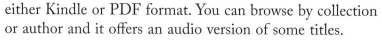

This app offers both an e-reader and a collection of 23,469 books. The site lets you read online, or download in either Kindle or PDF format. You can browse by collection or author and it offers an audio version of some titles.

Music

The Music app provides the means of accessing and managing your music. It offers:

Music

Don't forget

Windows 8 has two ways to play music – Windows Media Player and the Music app. However, for the Surface Tablet PC, with Windows RT, the music app is the only option provided.

- **Live streaming** – for this you must have access to your account. Live streaming is free for the first six months and then free for 10 hours a month thereafter

- **Xbox Music Pass** – with this option you pay for the pass but then are able to download music and listen to it wherever you choose. You are also able to sync the music with other Windows 8 devices. There is an option for a free trial

- **Purchase tracks on an individual basis** – these are then saved to your music folder and again always accessible

- **Manage any music stored in your Music library** – this is music you may have previously stored on another device and transferred to the Tablet PC

Selecting and Organizing

1   Open the Music app and you are presented with Now playing. Swipe left and select Start to choose a different artist or recording

Don't forget

Right click or swipe up in the Xbox music app to reveal the play, volume and playback controls.

2   The chosen artist and album is illustrated on Now playing

3 For a more comprehensive search, swipe or click the right-side Hotspot to reveal the Charms bar and select Search

4 You are offered a choice of albums and similar artists

5 Select a track or album and you then are able to purchase or add to a playlist

57

6 Select Playlist and you can then create your own list or lists of favorite music. Select your Playlist, once created, from beneath the Now playing window

7 New Smart DJ takes your choice of artist and creates a playlist of recordings of a similar era, artists or genre

Music from Other Sources

Music files are available from many sources. You may, for example, already have a selection of MP3 files from another computer or device. MP3 files can be downloaded from the Internet. To store these files on your computer you would need to use one of the following methods:

Internet Explorer

Search for free music files and follow the links provided. When you have located a suitable source follow the directions to download the music. The files will be downloaded into the Downloads folder from where you can transfer them to the Music folder.

1 Select the Desktop tile and click or tap the File Explorer icon, located on the Taskbar

2 Select the Downloads folder in the left panel to reveal its contents. Drag and drop the file or folder onto the Music folder. As you drag the folder you will see a representation of the move with the action

External Disk Drive

Copy files onto your computer using a memory (USB) stick or external CD drive.

1 Open the Desktop using the Desktop tile and select the File Explorer icon, to view the storage folders on your computer

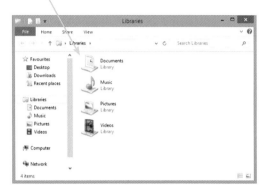

2 Click Computer in the left panel to see details of the disk drives. Each drive is allocated a sequential letter, with the C: drive being your main storage area

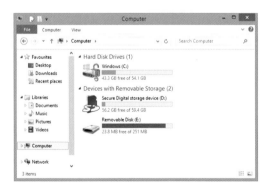

3 Connect a memory stick or external drive and the computer recognizes the device and displays its drive letter (E:), its status (removable) and the amount of space available (23.8 MB)

Don't forget

You cannot attach an external CD drive to the Microsoft Surface Tablet PC.

Don't forget

You can also copy files to your computer using SkyDrive to transfer them.

59

Hot tip

With a home network, you can share existing music files (see page 218 for more details).

...cont'd

Hot tip

The Address bar shows the location of the folder and the folder structure.

Hot tip

You can start to play your music in this view by double tapping a file. The computer switches to the Xbox view and displays the album sleeve if available.

4 Double click or tap the removable drive to view the contents. Similarly, double click or tap any folder to open it. In the example shown above, there are three artists' folders within the Music folder

5 Drag and drop an artist's folder into your Music folder on the left. The files will be copied onto the computer and can be played in the Music app

6 Double click or tap My Music to verify that the music has been copied

If you have used a memory stick as the source of your files, you should ensure that you use Windows 8 Drive Tools to eject the device:

1 Single click the drive so it is 'ticked' and select Manage from the Menu bar

2 Select Eject and you will be informed that it is safe to remove the drive

Games

Unlike previous versions of Windows, Windows 8 has no games initially installed, you have to use the Games app to locate, select and install them.

Hot tip

Playing games on your computer can be an easy way of becoming familiar with operations such as drag and drop, double click, etc.

Playing computer games online has become very popular, taking on a social aspect which is highly promoted and supported with the Xbox Games app. When you open the app you can:

- Create your own avatar, which is an animated persona with adjustable physique, clothes, hair, etc.

- Edit and share your profile with friends

- Invent or change your gamertag by which you will be identified in the on-line gaming world

- Invite friends to play by entering their gamertags

- Post messages and your gaming level achievements

However, to get started you simply need to select and download a game.

The Xbox Games app takes a similar approach to the Music app. It opens with Latest and Greatest. Scroll left and right to reveal further options and features. Click Windows Games Store to access the full inventory of games.

...cont'd

Hot tip

The Windows Games Store is not the Windows Store! When you search for a game, you are searching within the Games Store. You are redirected to the Windows Store to actually get the game.

With the Windows Games Store open:

1 Open the Charms bar and Search for free Solitaire. Select the Microsoft Solitaire Collection which is presented and tap Play

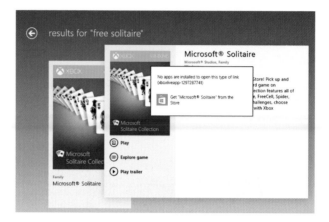

2 As this is the first time of use, the Games app recognizes that it is not installed and will redirect you to the Store. Tap the option to get Solitaire

3 Click Install to download the free program. You will see a series of small dots run across the top of the screen as it is installed and will be notified that it has installed successfully

The Solitaire Collection

This is a collection of single player card games, which will be familiar to many. The purpose of Solitaire, or Patience as it is often known, is to clear the board of cards. The Solitaire Collection offers five different games as well as a daily challenge.

Don't forget

You can change your Privacy settings at any time in your account settings.

1. Once installed, swipe or scroll right to see the new tile and select to view the collection

2. Choose a game. On first opening, you can choose to allow Microsoft to access your information

Hot tip

When you allow access, you will have a record of your scores and achievements, and can share this with others if you wish.

3. For each game (Klondike, Spider, FreeCell, Pyramid and TriPeaks) there are instructions on how to play, a scoreboard and a stepped Undo option

4. The Daily Challenge includes all five games, with a level of difficulty indicated. The challenge runs for a month and your progress through the period is shown with the value of 'coins' earned

5. Swipe or scroll right on the main Solitaire Collection screen, to change or create a new card Theme

6. You can also view a list of potential Awards, Medals and Daily Challenge Badges

Update the Apps

The Windows Store tile indicates if app updates are required (14 in our example). The list includes the apps that were installed when your Windows 8 was initially set up.

1. Tap the tile and then the indication Updates (14) on the Store screen in the top right corner (see page 52)

2. All the listed apps are currently selected (ticked) to be updated. Click or tap to deselect an app or select Install to update them all

3. A green status bar indicates the progress as each app is updated and you will be informed that the apps were installed

⊖ Installing apps

Your apps were installed.

4 Communicate

There are several ways to communicate using your PC. In this chapter we look at using Windows 8 Mail app and Internet Explorer to send and receive email. We also look at instant communication with Messaging and video programs such as Skype.

Electronic Mail

What is Email?

Email is the computerized way of sending memos and notes. Messages that you send are transmitted through a cable or phone connection to an Internet Service Provider (ISP). They are then forwarded to the recipient's ISP, where they will be held until the addressee connects and retrieves them.

You can store your email messages directly on your own PC. This is known as POP mail. Alternatively, the messages can be stored by your service provider. This is known as Web mail and uses Internet Explorer plus a mail program or app to access it (see page 68).

What You Need

1. Hardware that will allow you to connect to the Internet. This will be a modem (**mod**ulator/**dem**odulator), router or cable connection. The modem will require a telephone line, and can be either permanently connected (broadband or cable), or connected on demand (dial-up connection)

2. You will need to sign up with an Internet Service Provider (ISP) who will supply you with an email address that can be used for POP or Web mail

The usual form of an email address is:

individualname@network.com

name/number
e.g. sue.price

required
separator
(say it as AT)

address of network
e.g. gmail.com
or btinternet.com

3. Software to allow you to connect and send and receive mail. This may be provided by your ISP or you can use the Windows software – Internet Explorer and the Mail app

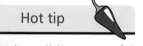

Hot tip

Web mail is very useful if you travel since it can be accessed from any computer.

Beware

It is important that you record any email address very carefully, taking particular note of dots (periods) and numbers. Also note that there are no spaces in an email address.

The Mail App

The Mail, People and Messaging apps together provide a comprehensive communications package. When you open Mail, you can use the information from the People app. When you open People, you can send an email using Mail. Similarly, when you open Messaging, you can use the contact details from People.

When you sign in to your computer using your Microsoft account, you are automatically signed in to Mail and Messaging. Both the Mail and Messaging tiles are live and indicate new activity on the account.

Don't forget

The People and Messaging apps are covered in greater detail later in the chapter.

1. Tap the Mail tile to view your email messages

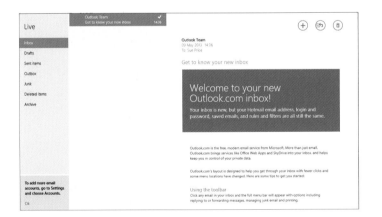

Hot tip

With a lower resolution screen, you may only see two panels.

2. You will see three panels – the left panel is the account (Live) panel with a list of folders. The middle panel lists mail in the Inbox (the highlighted folder) and the Reading panel showing the contents of the message, on the right

3. Scroll down the Reading panel for more of the text

Get an Email Address

Beware

Although your Microsoft account gives you an email address, you could find it very useful to have at least one other. Your Microsoft account is connected to the Windows Store, so you may wish to keep it separate from other correspondence. You might also find it useful to have one email address for family and friends, and one for business or shopping activities.

1. Open Internet Explorer and type www.google.com into the address bar and press Go or the Enter key

2. In the main Google search screen, click Gmail

3. Next, click the button to Create an account

4. Enter your details into the appropriate fields, pressing the Tab key to move from one to the next

5. Google will check your chosen username. If it is already in use, alternatives will be suggested

6. Complete the other fields, supplying a password, security question and typing the required text

7. Accept the terms of service and click Next. You can then add a photo of yourself before moving to the final step where your email address is confirmed

8. Select Continue to Gmail to view the welcome messages from Google

Hot tip

The Word Verification text is designed to prevent automated applications for email addresses.

Add the New Account

To register the new email address with the Mail app:

1. Open the Mail app and swipe from the right or right-click to reveal the Charms bar and select Settings

2. Choose Accounts and then Add an account

3. Many of the usual online account providers are listed. Select as appropriate, or if yours is not listed, select Other account

4. You will need to enter your username and password, then click Connect

5. Read and check the details of how Google can interact with the Microsoft Live.com account. Then click Connect

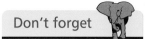

Don't forget

With Mail as the active app, Settings applies automatically to the options within Mail.

Don't forget

You should make careful note of all your email addresses and of any associated passwords.

69

...cont'd

6 Microsoft then asks for permission to access details within the Gmail account. Click Allow access

← Connecting to a service

Google   Sue Price

Microsoft is requesting permission to:

▸ Manage your contacts
▸ View basic information about your account
· Perform these operations when I'm not using the application

Microsoft   **Microsoft**
             Learn more

Allow access   No thanks

7 The final step informs you that the account is being set up. Click Done to return to Mail

← You're ready to go

We're setting things up now, so it might be a few minutes before you see any changes.

Add more accounts in settings
You can add more accounts or change these connection settings at any time in the settings for this app.

Done

8 Mail now shows messages from the Gmail account, with both accounts now listed at the bottom of the Accounts panel

Hot tip

Windows 8 lets you add two other types of email accounts – EAS and iMAP – in addition to web-based email accounts.

Don't forget

The Mail app is designed to let you view each account separately, so it's easy to manage several accounts.

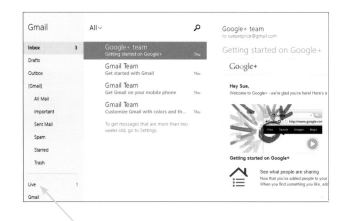

9 Click Live to switch accounts and view messages in the Live.com account

The Mail Folders

The Mail app uses a folder system to organize your email, much the same as you would use to manage your correspondence in an office. You will find that all email programs have a very similar folder structure.

With two accounts now registered to the Mail app, you will notice slight differences in the way the folders are named and organized, according to the account selected.

Live	
Inbox	
Flagged	**1**
Drafts	**1**
Sent	
Outbox	
Junk	
Deleted	

Gmail	
Inbox	**3**
Drafts	
Outbox	
[Gmail]	
All Mail	
Important	
Sent Mail	
Spam	**1**
Starred	
Trash	

Hot tip

The folder structure reflects the folder structure of the online accounts at Live.com and Gmail.com.

Hot tip

The folders are shown under the account name. To view the contents of any folder, simply click on the folder you wish to view in the Folder list pane.

The Inbox

When you open the Mail app, any messages waiting on the server will be downloaded to the Inbox. They will remain in this folder until you move or delete them, allowing you to read them, and if required, reply to or forward them. The number on the Inbox indicates the number of unread messages in the Inbox.

The Outbox

When you create an email and click Send, the email will be transferred to the Outbox. Mail is usually sent immediately, but if you have a connection delay, the Outbox will display the number of emails waiting to go.

The email will be sent from (and uses the email address of) the account that is currently being viewed.

...cont'd

Sent Items
A copy of all email sent will be put in your Sent Items folder, allowing you to reference them later if necessary.

Deleted Items
When you delete messages, they are transferred to the Deleted Items folder, and will remain there until you decide to empty the folder.

Drafts
You can store unfinished email in the Drafts folder, or save messages that you have written but do not wish to send immediately. The message can be completed and sent from the Drafts folder.

Junk or Spam Email
This folder is used to store junk or unwanted email. You can move selected messages to the Junk folder yourself, but you will find that some 'suspect' email is stored there automatically. You should check the Junk folder occasionally for mis-sorted items.

> Sue Price (dp)   13/05/2013 15:12
> to Sue Price
>
> **This message is marked as junk email.**
> All links, images and attachments have been disabled to help protect you. If you trust the sender, move the message out of your junk emails and we'll restore it to how we found it.
> Fw: Voyage Prive offers luxury travel at up to 70% off

When an item is placed in the Junk folder, you are informed that all links have been disabled. If you trust the sender, move it to the Inbox and all links, images and attachments will be reinstated.

1 Select the message and right click or swipe up to reveal the Apps bar. Tap the Not junk icon and the message is automatically transferred to the Inbox

Not junk

Receiving Email

With a broadband connection, any email held on the server for you will be downloaded to your computer when you open the Mail app.

1 New messages are saved into your Inbox, with the number of new messages indicated

2 The Inbox lists all incoming messages. To view only those still to be read, click the down arrow next to All and select Unread

3 Messages of particular importance can be flagged (or starred in Gmail) for later action. Select the message and then swipe up or right-click to reveal the App bar. Tap or click the Flag icon

4 Tap or left-click Flagged in the folder panel to view only flagged messages. Tap or click the Inbox to see all messages

5 The message header indicates an attachment with a paperclip symbol (see page 77)

6 Messages are held in the Inbox for two weeks. For older messages, reveal the Charms bar and choose Settings

7 Select the account and then your choice of period

Don't forget

To remove the Flag from marked messages, reverse the process. The icon changes to Remove flag.

73

Hot tip

Click or tap the text at the bottom of the Inbox to go straight to the option to get older email messages.

To get messages that are more than two weeks old, go to Settings

Create an Email Message

1. Open the Mail app and click on the Plus button on the top right of the main screen (or press Ctrl + N)

2. A New Message window will open. Click in the To: line and type the email address of the recipient

3. Click Cc and add the addresses of those you wish to send Carbon (or Courtesy) copies

4. Tap or click the Subject line and type the subject of your message

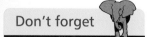

5. Click in the typing area and type your message. Reveal the App bar to make changes to the text size and font, add elements such as bold and italic or even Emoticons

6. The standard text functions copy and paste, (see page 138) are available. Click the More icon for functions such as Insert link, Undo and Redo

7. When finished, click on Send. The message will be transferred to the Outbox and sent immediately

Manage Your Email

When you start getting lots of email, use the facilities within Mail to organize it. To create storage folders:

1 Reveal the App bar and select the Folder options icon. Select New folder for it to appear in the main folder list

2 In the new window, type the Folder name then click Create folder

Hot tip

Select Subfolder if you wish the folder to be stored within another, for example the Inbox.

3 The new folder will appear in the Folder list on the left

4 Select email that you wish to put in the new folder and swipe up to reveal the App bar

5 Click or tap the Move icon. The screen becomes grayed out with only the folder list active. Select the folder and the item is moved immediately

Conversation Streams

Messages in the Inbox are grouped by conversation, which means that all messages relating to a specific email are grouped together. This is a setting in the Mail Options that is initially set to On. The original email and any further replies from your computer are also listed in the Sent folder.

Hot tip

To delete email, you can select the item and click the Trash can. Alternatively, you could reveal the App bar, choose Select all and then tap the trash can. You can also use Folder options to empty the folder.

Reply and Forward

Using Reply has two main advantages: the person receiving the reply gets a copy of the message he or she sent, so reminding them of the topic and details. It also reuses their address, taking away the need to find or check for the correct address.

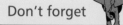 With the email message open, simply click on the Reply button

| Reply |
| Reply all |
| Forward |

The window changes to allow you to add your text, with the original message lower down. The Subject bar shows Re: to indicate a reply

Sue Price
sue.j.price@live.com

Re: Rotary meeting

To
Michael Price

Cc

Show more

Hi Mike,
Thanks for the invitation. I would love to come.
I know someone else who is really interested to hear him talk. I shall ask her along.
Sue

Sent from Windows Mail

From: Michael Price
Sent: Wednesday, 15 May 2013 14:40
To: Sue Price

Hi Sue,
At our meeting on Wednesday Tom Jones will be speaking about his travels.

Would you like to come and bring a friend?

Please let me know either way.

Regards, Mike....

When finished, click on Send and the message will be sent in the usual way

Forward

Forward uses the same process as Reply, but this time you must supply one or more addresses. The letters Fw: indicate the message is being forwarded. When you forward a message, any attachments that came with the original message are also forwarded.

Fw: Rotary meeting

Hi Chris
I had this invitation from Mike. Would you like to go?
Sue
Sent from Windows Mail

Attachments

One of the benefits of sending email is to be able to send or receive other information, such as photos or an event schedule, along with the email. These are known as attachments.

Attached files could be documents created with a word processor, a spreadsheet with lists and calculations or photos downloaded from your digital camera.

Sending an Attachment

1 Create your email as you would normally. You can add the attachment at any point

2 Select the paperclip on the toolbar. This will open a window into your Libraries

3 Select the folder, for example Documents, then the file and click Attach

4 You now return to your message, and the header section shows an attachment with the file name and size

5 Complete the message and press Send

Beware

When you send an attachment, check the size of the file. Data files such as spreadsheets and documents are usually quite small, but photos can be very large. If your recipient has a slow connection it can take a long time to download.

Receiving an Attachment

If the email has a file attached, it will be indicated on the message by the paperclip symbol:

1. Open the message. You will see the name of the attached file(s) and the size and the option to download

2. Click or tap the attachment name to open. Choose Open and the file opens in the associated program. In the example shown it opens in the Desktop environment in Word

3. Choose Open with to select the program yourself. This option applies principally to photo files, but you can select More options for other program

To work with the attached file, for example a text document or spreadsheet, you will need to save it to disk.

4. Select Save and you are transferred to the Files/folder view. Navigate the folders for the required location and click Save

Edit the Attachment

To be able to work with attachments, the file type must be registered on your computer. This means that it will have an associated application. For example, files with .doc or .docx as part of the filename are associated and opened with Word, files with the .xls or .xlsx file extension are associated with Excel spreadsheets. To view the attachment:

How do you want to open this file?

☑ Use this application for all .doc files

Keep using Word (desktop)

Internet Explorer

Notepad

Paint

Windows Photo Viewer

Look for an app in the Store

1 Close Mail or just select the Windows key to return to the Start screen and then select the Desktop tile

Desktop

2 Click the File Explorer tile and locate the file that you have just saved into the folder

Don't forget

If you know which app or program is required to view the attachment, select the program on the Start screen and use the program's utilities to locate the file.

Name	Date modified	Type
📊 Holiday Schedule	05/05/2013 10:56	Microsoft Excel W...
🖼 image003	16/05/2013 09:36	JPG File
📊 InventoryList	05/05/2013 10:56	Microsoft Excel W...
📄 Madeira Trip	05/05/2013 10:56	Microsoft Word D...
📊 Music_List	05/05/2013 10:56	Microsoft Excel W...
📄 NADFAS Gilbert White and Chawton ...	16/05/2013 09:36	Microsoft Word 9...
📊 Our Charity Donations picture show	05/05/2013 10:56	Microsoft PowerP...
📄 Our Charity Donations show	05/05/2013 10:56	Microsoft PowerP...

Favourites — Desktop, Downloads, Recent places
Libraries — Documents, Music, Pictures, Videos
Libraries ▸ Documents
17 items   1 item selected 95.0 KB   Library includes: 2 locations

3 Double tap or double click it. It should open in the associated application. You will still need to click Enable editing to make any changes

4 If, unusually, your computer cannot read the file, you may have to ask the sender to resend it in a different format, or search the Internet for a suitable application or solution

Security Settings

There are many security functions built into Windows 8, including passwords, firewalls and file encryption (see page 222). Email also has a set of safety options, but to view and change the settings you need to go to the email server itself.

1. Open Internet Explorer and type the address of your account supplier in the address bar, for example www.live.com

2. Select Settings and then More email settings to view the range of controls available

Outlook | ⌄

Options Inbox > Options

Managing your account	Preventing junk email
Account details (password, addresses, time zone)	Filters and reporting
Your email accounts	Safe and blocked senders
Email forwarding	
Sending automated holiday replies	**Customising Outlook**
POP and deleting downloaded messages	Advanced privacy settings
Messaging history	Language
Create an Outlook alias	Keyboard shortcuts
Rename your email address	Rules for sorting new messages
Upgrade to Ad-free Outlook	Flagging
	Instant actions

3. Click, for example, Filters and reporting where you can change the filter from Standard to Exclusive

Outlook | ⌄

Filters and reporting Inbox > Options > Filters and reporting

Choose a junk email filter

Select the filter level you want to apply to incoming messages.

● Standard – Most junk emails are sent to the junk email folder.

○ Exclusive – Everything is sent to the junk email folder except messages from your contacts and safe senders, Outlook service announcements, and alerts that you signed up for.

Note: You should occasionally check your junk email folder to make sure that good messages don't get put there by mistake.

4. Use the options under Safe and blocked senders to choose who is considered safe and who should be blocked completely

Your Contacts

The People app organizes all details of your contacts, providing a one-stop-shop for information that can be used for email, phone and other contact means.

The People app can be synchronized with your Windows 8 mobile phone so that your contacts' details are always to hand.

It works with the Mail app, and provides a direct link to the Mail app.

1 Open the People app, swipe up to reveal the App bar and select New contact

2 Complete the details, using the keyboard Tab key to move from field to field

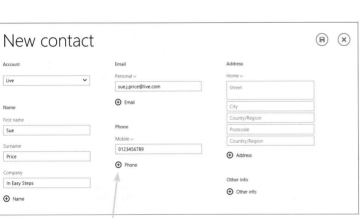

3 Click the Plus sign to add extra fields, for example a second email address or phone number

4 Click the arrow next to the category to change the designation, for example from Mobile phone to Home phone

5 Click the Save button when finished or the X to discard the changes

82

With your contacts' details completed, the People app, once set up properly, provides the swiftest way to communicate:

- **Send message** – this option offers Messaging as the means of communication and uses the contact's mobile or cell phone number. You may need to tap the down arrow to invoke the app. (see opposite for using Messaging)

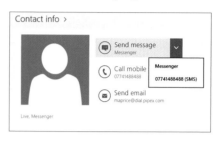

- **Call mobile** – with no suitable app to use, you are redirected to the Windows Store. The Store opens with appropriate apps from which to choose

- **Send email** – this opens the Mail app with the To field already completed

Live Chat

The Messaging app can be used to contact friends and create an online conversation.

1 Open the app and start to type the person's name and select as appropriate. Alternatively, tap the Plus sign to open the People app for you to select the contact

Hot tip

When you sign in to your account with Live.com, you are automatically signed in to messaging services.

2 Once selected, the contact's name appears in Messaging, highlighted. Add your message at the bottom of the screen and press the Enter key to send

Hot tip

You are informed if your contact is unavailable, but you are still able to send a message.

83

3 To invite a friend, swipe up or right mouse click to reveal the App bar, click the Invite icon and follow the prompts

Hot tip

If you have a Facebook account, you can use your contacts from there. Swipe to reveal the Charms bar, select Settings, Accounts and Add an account. Select Facebook and follow the instructions.

4 Click the Status icon to Invisible if you wish to be undisturbed

Video Contact

With a webcam and microphone, you can use your computer as a live video link to friends and family. You could use a Live.com ID and use Messaging which has a video option. However, we will use Skype, with its video link capability.

1 Search for Skype in the Windows Store for the version suitable for Windows 8 (RT)

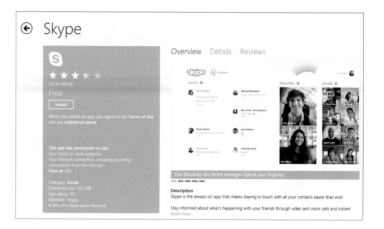

84

2 Click the Install button and once installed, return to the Start screen and select the new Skype tile

3 Follow the prompts to allow Skype to use the webcam and microphone, and to allow the app to run in the background

4 You can then choose to use an existing Skype account or create a new one

Already using Skype?   New to Skype?

Merge with your existing Skype account to access your credit and all your contacts in one place.

Welcome! It's quick and easy to join

I have a Skype account   I'm new to Skype

5 As a first step, check out your system using the Echo/Sound test to confirm the camera and microphone are enabled and working correctly

Known contacts will be listed under People. To add a contact:

6 Swipe up to reveal the App bar and select Add contact. This opens Search on the Charms bar where you can enter a name or Skype username

7 Select the contact name, and then Add to contacts. You will be prompted to send a Contact request message

8 To talk to a contact, click their name and then either the green Call button or the Video button. Press the red receiver to hang up

9 Select your account icon to change your settings for Available or Invisible

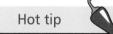

Don't forget

Skype searches your People app for the contact. It will also search its own Directory, if required, for matching names.

Hot tip

For security reasons, you must invite people to join you, so you can be sure who you are actually in contact with.

85

Travel and Email

With web-based email such as Live.com and Gmail.com accounts, you can use Internet Explorer to access your email from any computer, for example a friend's, or at a coffee shop or library. The mail is stored on a server by your ISP, allowing you to access this account from anywhere in the world, thus keeping in touch when you travel.

By using Internet Explorer to read your mail on a different computer, the messages are left on the server and only downloaded when you return to your own computer and use a program such as the Mail app to synchronize your email.

When you look at mail on the Web you will find that the facilities and processes are very much the same as those provided by the Mail app.

Don't forget

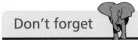

If you are paying for a dial-up connection when traveling, you will pay for the time spent working with Web mail.

Hot tip

Web mail can be subject to a great deal of spam (unsolicited mail). Most service providers give you a way to report it.

1 To access your account, open Internet Explorer and type www.live.com (or www.gmail.com, www.outlook.com etc.) into the address bar. Supply your user name and password to sign in

2 You can navigate the folders as you do in the Mail app – just click the folder that you want to open

3 Use the ⊕ New icon to start a new message

5 Surfing the Web

We look at the Internet, follow links between sites and pages (surfing the Web), learn how to locate answers to your questions and find information. Learn how to install updates and enable settings to keep your Internet browsing safe and secure.

What is the Internet?

The Internet is made up of millions of computers across the world that use common data and communications standards and cooperate with each other to exchange information.

Hot tip

The key attribute of the Internet is that there is no owner or central authority. It is bound only by the standards and policies that have been mutually accepted as the network evolved from the original academic and research based network.

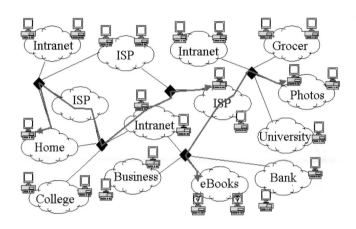

The computers may belong to governments, universities, businesses or private individuals. Through the shared information exchange this creates, Internet users can:

Hot tip

Security on the Internet is explained on page 104.

- Connect via ordinary PCs and local phone numbers
- Exchange email with friends and colleagues
- Post and update information for others to access
- Access text, sound, photographic images and video
- Get a world-wide perspective on what's happening

The data standard that makes the Internet as we see it today is HyperText Transfer Protocol (HTTP). This is a means of defining an electronic document known as a Web Page that can be displayed on a PC monitor. It contains Hyperlinks to associated web pages (forming a local website) and to other web pages and websites on computers across the Internet. These websites are collectively referred to as the World Wide Web, or the Web for short.

Hot tip

Web pages use color and can contain text, any style and any size, pictures, animated graphics, videos and sound (music or speech).

To access the websites, display the web pages and follow the hyperlinks use a web browser such as Microsoft's Internet Explorer, provided with Windows 8.

Your PC must have a connection to the Internet.
This requires an account with an Internet Service Provider,
and a modem or router to connect to the telephone or cable
system. Your PC supplier may already have set this up for
you, or may have provided CDs and information for you to
set up your own account with one of the popular ISPs such
as AOL, Earthlink or Verizon.

To open your browser:

1   Click or tap the Internet Explorer tile
     on the Start screen

2   The browser opens full screen, with the
     default web page, often the home page
     for the ISP, or in this instance the MSN home page

Hot tip

Windows 8 computers
have two versions
of Internet Explorer.
One is accessed from
the Start screen, with
a second version
available on the
Desktop. The Desktop
version will be familiar
to users of previous
editions of Internet
Explorer.

The Browser Window

Web page   Information   Search   MSN page
name   categories   bar   options

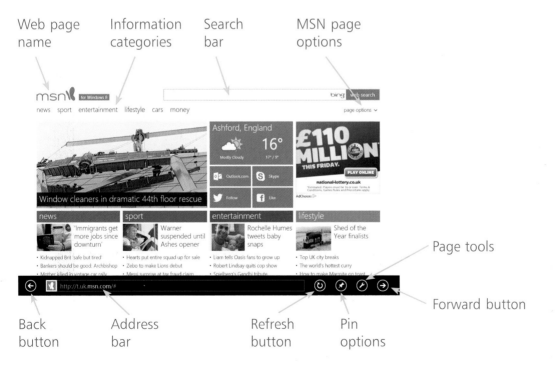

Page tools

Forward button

Back   Address   Refresh   Pin
button   bar   button   options

Web Addresses

When you visit a web page using your browser, the Address bar shows the web address. For example, the web address for the New York Times World news is:

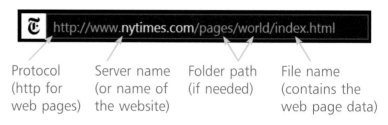

Protocol
(http for
web pages)

Server name
(or name of
the website)

Folder path
(if needed)

File name
(contains the
web page data)

To visit a web page, click in the Address bar and type the address. You needn't type the http:// since Internet Explorer assumes web pages by default.

To visit the home page for a website, just type the server or website name, leaving out the folder path and the web page name. You can even leave out the www. For example, you'd enter ineasysteps.com to visit the home page for the In Easy Steps website:

① The Hand pointer appears when you move the mouse over a hyperlink, and the destination is shown in a small window

---

Hot tip

The web address is the URL, or Uniform Resource Locator.

Hot tip

The end part of the website name indicates the type of organization that owns the website:

.com — Commercial
.edu — Academic
.gov — Government
.org — Non-profit
.net — Network

The above are used for Global or USA websites, but the ending can also indicate the specific country, for example:

.com.au — Australia
.ca — Canada
.net.in — India
.co.nz — New Zealand
.co.za — South Africa
.co.uk — UK

Hot tip

Hyperlinks are often underlined, and may change color when the mouse is on them.

Navigating the Web

Hyperlinks are used in several ways to help you navigate your way around a website and across the Web.

1 Go to the Home page for the current website

2 Click a category for a list of specific quick links

Don't forget

The hyperlinks on web pages provide the main way in which you explore the World Wide Web.

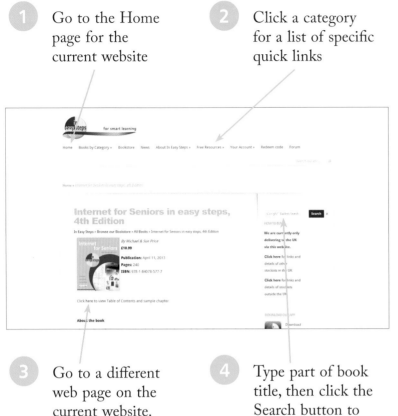

3 Go to a different web page on the current website. This link opens in a separate app, Reader (see page 100 for details)

4 Type part of book title, then click the Search button to look for another title or author

Hot tip

Images can also be used as hyperlinks. For example, if you point to the image of the book on this website, the hand pointer appears, and the link will take you to the larger version of the image in a separate window.

5 Swipe up or scroll to see the rest of the information. Stretch or pinch to zoom in and out

6 Click the Back and Forward buttons to switch between web pages you have visited previously

Choose Your Home Page

Windows 8 has, to some extent, taken away the need to create your own Home page by presenting tiles on the Start screen that cover typical Home page items, such as local weather, news, and a dedicated Search engine tile (Bing).

You can only set the Home page in the Desktop version of Internet Explorer.

If you close Internet Explorer, the Home page is presented when you re-open it. If you shut down the computer with Internet Explorer still open, when you restart, it will remember and open with the last website viewed.

When you open Internet Explorer for the very first time, you will most likely see a version of the image shown on page 89, the Microsoft Network (MSN) page. It offers up-to-date news, weather and other articles. This is an example of a Home page.

You can decide for yourself just what you would like as your Home page when you open the program. You might for example, wish to open with a site such as the New York Times or the BBC or create your own with links to local news and websites.

A further option, and probably the most usual, is to open with a Search engine such as Google or Bing, as most of the time you will search for websites, rather than type in their web address. To set your Home page:

1   Click the Desktop tile and then the Internet Explorer icon on the Taskbar

2   Type the required address, e.g. www.google.com into the Address bar (which in this version of Internet Explorer is at the top of the screen) and press Enter

| ← → | http://www.google.co.uk/ | ρ ∼ ¢ | Google | × | ⌂ ★ ☼ |

3   With the required website showing, press and hold, or right mouse click, the Home button and select Add or change Home page

Menu bar
Favourites bar
Command bar
Status bar

Lock the toolbars
Show tabs on a separate row
Add or change home page

4   Select Use this webpage as your only home page and click Yes to finish

Add or Change Home Page

Would you like to use the following as your home page?

http://www.google.com/

◉ Use this webpage as your only home page
○ Add this webpage to your home page tabs

Yes   No

Searching for Web Pages

1 For a general search topic such as Information for Seniors, you will find many web pages – in this case over 32 million. As you type your search criteria, search engines such as Google suggest related topics

 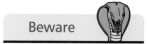

2 Make the search more specific, for example "Financial Planning for Seniors", to get fewer matches – in this case about 91,000

3 To find a particular website, you need a more exact search topic, such as Education for seniors in Denver

4 Click the link on the results list to visit the website

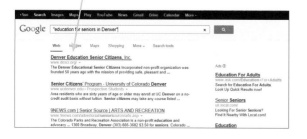

Tabbed Browsing

You will probably find more than one site of interest on a topic. To make comparing information easier, Internet Explorer offers tabs. You can have a whole series of tabs, each showing a separate web page.

Hot tip

When you open the browser, it will have one browsing tab which displays your Home page.

1 With Internet Explorer open, swipe down or right-click to reveal the Tab bar. Initially, only the current screen is shown. Tap or click the Plus button to open a new tab

Hot tip

With a mouse or keyboard attached, you can right-click the link and choose Open in new tab. It is also possible to press and hold the link to reveal the same menu option, but it does take some practice.

2 When you add a new tab, Internet Explorer reveals your Frequent and Favorites sites. Scroll to select from these sites, or type the web address into the Address bar underneath

Don't forget

In the Desktop edition of Internet Explorer, the tabs are visible all the time towards the top of the window. Just click the tab to select. See page 96.

3 To switch between websites, swipe or drag down to reveal the Tab bar

4 Close individual tabs by revealing the tab bar and tapping the X (Close) button

5 Drag down from the very top to the bottom of the screen, with gesture or mouse, to close the program completely

Returning to a Website

Once you've found some useful websites, you will probably want to make sure you can return to them in future. Internet Explorer offers several ways to keep track of your surfing.

 1 To go back to the previous web page or the results list, click the Back button

 **2** Click the right arrow at the end of the Address bar to go forward again to revisit a site during the current browsing session

Favorites or Bookmarks

When you've found a website you might visit frequently, you can save it as one of your favorites.

3 With the website displayed, reveal the App bar and click or tap the Pin symbol and choose Add to favorites. Links to these websites will be available when you open a new tab

When you have a topic where you might want to do more in-depth research, or save a series of similar websites, use the Favorites folders. To access, manage and organize your Favorites folders, you will need to use the Desktop version of Internet Explorer as described on the next page.

4 Click the Spanner icon and select View on Desktop

Manage Your Favorites

Windows 8 provides two versions of Internet Explorer 10. The Start screen app, described and illustrated so far, uses the tools and settings from the Desktop version, as shown previously in setting the Home page. To manage your Favorites:

Hot tip

Favorite websites listed in either version of Internet Explorer will be listed in Favorites.

1 Open the Desktop version of Internet Explorer and select the Favorites icon

Don't forget

The Start screen app version of Internet Explorer doesn't use folders, you just scroll through the list of Favorites.

2 Select a website you wish to add and click or tap Add to favorites

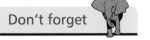

3 Initially, the suggested folder is Favorites. To create a subfolder within Favorites, select New folder

4 Name the folder and click or tap Create. The new folder will be listed. You can drag and drop any previously, saved sites into the folder

5 To visit a web page, click Favorites and choose an entry from the list. To open the website, but keep your current page visible, click the arrow to Open in a new tab

6 To display the list continually, click the green arrow at the top of Favorites to Pin the Favorites Center to the window

History

1 Use the History tab to show recently-visited web pages. Choose the week or day, then the folder. This expands to show pages visited at that website

2 Click a page to revisit that particular topic

3 History is organized by date, but you can also list it by site, most visited or you can search History for specific topics

Refresh
Internet Explorer will occasionally be unable to display a particular web page, or will take much longer to display it than expected. Both versions have a Refresh button which will initiate another attempt to contact the website.

Desktop IE

Start screen app

Don't forget

The History tab is most useful when you have visited a website and forgotten the name or exactly which links you followed to find it.

97

Hot tip

The Start screen version of Internet Explorer doesn't offer History in the same way, just frequently-visited.

Save Picture from Web Page

You may want to download a copy of an image that you find on a web page. Perhaps, for example, you want to look more closely at Leonardo Da Vinci's Last Supper.

1. Open Google, select Images, type a brief description and then click Search Images. Click or tap Search tools to specify a larger image

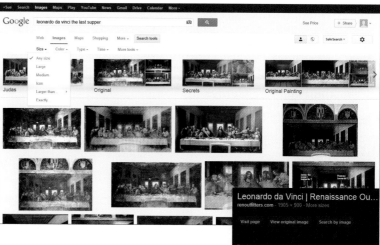

2. When the results are displayed, choose a suitable image and click to display the web page containing it

3. Click View original image to display the image alone

4. To save the image to your hard disk, right-click the image or press and hold until the menu appears, and select Save to picture library

5. The image will be saved to your Pictures folder

Save Text from Web Page

Information from a web page can be saved to a document for later use.

1 Open Internet Explorer on the Desktop and display the required information

2 With the mouse or keypad, select the text. Click at the beginning of the text and drag across to select it. It will be highlighted

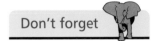

Hot tip

The Start menu IE app only offers to copy the information.

Don't forget

By selecting the text, you can limit the selection to the details you actually want.

3 Right-click the text and select Copy. The text is saved into memory and can be pasted into a Word document or to OneNote

Print a Web page

1 Use the Print option from the right-click menu as shown above. This will take you to the Print window where you can select the printer, number of copies, etc.

2 Alternatively, click the Tools button and select Print > Print preview from there

3 Press Ctrl + P to print from the Start screen app

Hot tip

Use Print preview from Tools to see what exactly you will get when you print. Print preview of the Leonardo Da Vinci page from Wikipedia shows 10 pages of print material.

Online PDF Documents

When you visit a website you will often find reference documents in the PDF format.

1 Visit the website www.keswick.org/what-to-do/walking-routes/
Select a walk that interests you, for example Brund Fell Walk

2 Click the title. You will be asked if you wish to Open or Save the document

3 Choose Open if you just wish to browse the document. Choose Save if you wish to read it offline later

4 Reader offers a number of tools, visible when you swipe or click to reveal the App bar

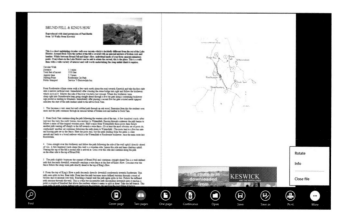

5 Use the Find tool to locate specific text in the document. Click More to rotate the screen and close the file

6 When you select to Save the document it will be saved into the Downloads folder. Click View downloads, or Open folder, to open and view the contents of the Downloads folder

The brund fell.pdf download has completed.   Open ▼   Open folder   View downloads   ✕

6 Double-click the document to open it with Reader

To open the PDF file in the Start screen environment:

1 Swipe up to reveal the App bar and choose All apps

2 Select Reader. When it opens, it lists Recent documents. You must select Browse and navigate the folders to locate the Downloads folder where the other files are stored

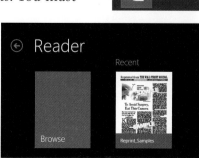

TV Online

NBC, ABC and many other TV channels allow you to watch and listen to TV from the previous week, or with many programs and series, from a longer period.

1 Go to the NBC website at www.nbc.com and select Shows for a list of current, favorite and classic videos

2 Alternatively, select Video for full episodes of Clips of current or topical programs

3 Select Schedule for a list of programs and times for the current and following day

Hot tip

These videos can be watched online (streamed) or even downloaded to your computer or other hardware, such as the Apple iPad.

Don't forget

When you sign up with an ISP, you will be allowed a download limit. If you watch or download video from the Internet regularly, you should monitor your usage.

Beware

Television programs and films are subject to copyright.
You may find that if you try to view your favorite program when you are away from your home country that the program is blocked.

To view television in the UK or other countries, go to the Windows Store and search for iplayer. Download and install, for example, the app TunerFree.

1 Open the app and you can decide which channels to select. You are advised that not all channels are available in all countries. Press Continue

2 Select, for example, BBC One and then scroll through to select a program from those offered. iPlayer is started and the usual video controls are enabled

3 To add more channels to view, swipe to reveal the Charms bar, and choose Settings, then TunerFree Channels. The complete list is displayed

4 Choose TunerFree Options for the possibility to purchase a licence to support the program's development

Hot tip

Go to the website for a broadcaster in your region to watch live TV. For example, visit bbc.co.uk to watch United Kingdon programs.

Don't forget

Currently there are just two apps that offer television streaming - TunerFree and TVCatchup. Both apps offer several tv stations, other functions and features may vary.

103

Beware

Sometimes the demands of the video exceed the broadband speed, causing disrupted action especially at busy times.

Internet Security

When you are surfing the Internet, you run the risk of infecting your computer with undesirable programs. Antivirus software helps prevent or remedy such problems. Windows 8 and Windows RT have Windows Defender built in, to protect your system from malicious software, viruses and spyware.

To open Windows Defender and check your safety status:

1   From the Start screen, reveal the Charms bar and select Search. Type Defender into the Search field

2   Select Windows Defender in the results. It will open on the Desktop, displaying your current status

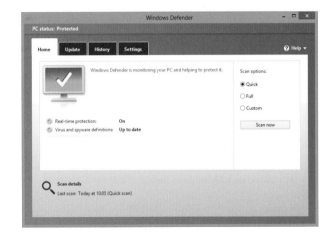

Windows Defender keeps constant track of unfamiliar or suspicious software and checks it against a database to ensure that no harmful activity can take place. It performs a scan and updates automatically on a regular, scheduled basis. However, if you wish you can initiate a scan by selecting Scan now, choosing Quick, Full or Custom.

If the scan reveals a problem, you can view details of the quarantined item by selecting the History tab and then deleting the item.

Similarly, you can initiate an Update of virus and spyware definitions by clicking the Update tab.

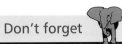

Don't forget

Malicious software, (known as 'malware' for short) is designed to get into a computer and disrupt the operating system and/or damage data. Spyware is written to access user's private information without the user being aware. Both types are often designed to replicate and spread like a 'virus' through insecure websites, emails and networks. Windows Defender uses red, amber and green color coding to indicate the security level of your computer.

Hot tip

You could run Windows Defender if you receive an email that you think is suspicious or from an obscure source.

Windows SmartScreen, new to Windows 8, warns you about
suspect apps, phishing and malware attacks. It identifies sites
that have a questionable reputation or have been reported as
unsafe.

To check your SmartScreen settings:

1 Reveal the Charms bar, select Settings and type
Action Center into the Search box

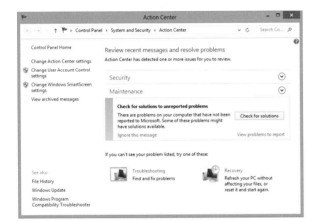

Don't forget

If the SmartScreen
filter detects that you
are viewing an unsafe
website, you will get a
warning message.

105

2 Click the option to Change Windows SmartScreen
settings to view the current settings

Hot tip

You might find an
alternative antivirus
program installed on
your computer by your
supplier.

3 Select Cancel to leave the settings unchanged, and
only change the setting if you are completely sure

Manage Your Browser

Delete Browsing History

Internet Explorer keeps track of your activities on the Internet, creating a Browsing History as you work. In some circumstances, such as an Internet café, or on someone else's PC, it's a good idea to remove your browsing history when finished. To delete your browsing history:

1 Select Search from the Charms bar, then Settings and type Internet options into the Search field

2 In the Browsing history section select Delete

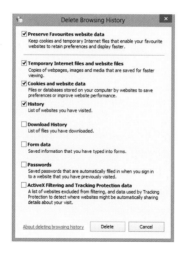

3 Add or remove ticks for each category as you feel is appropriate. Then click or tap Delete to apply the changes

Pop-up Blocker

Pop-ups are annoying little advertisements that may appear on the screen when you browse the Internet and it's best to ignore them. By default, the Pop-up blocker is turned on.

To view or change the setting for the Pop-up Blocker:

1 Click the Privacy tab in the Internet Options window as shown previously

2 Tap Settings to allow exceptions. Note that you will be informed if a pop-up is blocked

Family Safety

Use Family Safety to manage how children or grandchildren use the computer. You can set time limits, control the games they play, sites they visit or apps they can download.

1 You must be signed on with an Administrator account. You also need to create a User account for the child or each child (See Chapter 12)

2 Swipe to reveal the Charms bar, select Settings and type Family Safety into the Search field

3 Select the child's account to open the User Settings window to view the available settings and restrictions

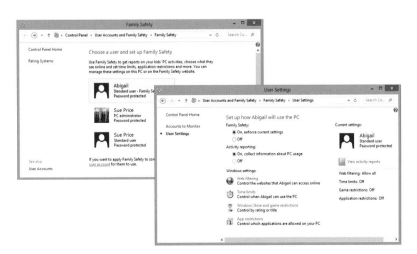

Hot tip

You can create a new account from the Family Safety window.

107

Hot tip

Children's safety when using the Internet is extremely important. For more information and guidance on the available controls visit windows.microsoft. com and search for Family Safety.

Useful Websites

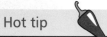

Hot tip

Here are just a few websites that may help you get started with surfing the Internet. You can find more in our book *Internet for Seniors in easy steps*.

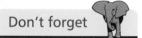

Don't forget

Help for using your computer system can be found at: support.microsoft.com or at: windows.microsoft.com

1 The American Association of Retired Persons (AARP) can be found at http://www.aarp.org/ and has a wide array of articles and links designed for the over 50s. It offers a magazine, discounts and advice on health, Medicare and Social Security

2 At www.usa.gov/Topics/Seniors.shtml you will find links to resources on consumer protection, education, volunteering, health, housing and many other topics

3 The Internet Senior Success Center at www.internetseniorsuccess.com/seniorsites.htm lists top websites related to seniors and those age over 50

6 Shopping on the Web

Another great activity on the Internet is shopping. You can buy just about anything, from automobiles to groceries. You can even take part in auctions. We cover what you have to do, and what you must look out for.

Sign Up for Offers

If you've not yet made an Internet purchase, and you are concerned about privacy or giving out credit card information, take advantage of offers and the latest information that is available without charge and with no need to provide much in the way of personal detail.

For example, sign up to a major department store such as Macy's for email notices announcing their latest offers and new arrivals.

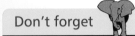
1 Start Internet Explorer and type www.macys.com into the address bar. Click the option to sign up for emails

2 Supply the required details, confirm that you are over 18 and click or tap Submit

3 At other shops, for example Marks and Spencers in the UK at www.marksandspencer.com you can sign up for a newsletter with just an email address

Newspapers

The Internet allows you to view online versions of newspapers, both national and international.

 Visit a website such as www.onlinenewspapers.com/ to access newspaper websites worldwide

2 Select a country/state to view a list of locally-published newspapers, organized alphabetically

3 Choose, for example, The Chicago Tribune www.chicagotribune.com
You can read the latest news, sport, business, etc. for free, register to get greater access or buy a monthly subscription for full access

Beware

For crosswords on many newspaper sites, you may need to take out a paying subscription.

Don't forget

You can pin a favorite site such as a newspaper to the Start screen.

eBooks

There's a collection of nearly 42,000 free electronic books in the Project Gutenberg website at http://www.gutenberg.org/

 Enter the book or author details into the Search box and click Go

 Scroll sideways through the authors' titles in the Results window for other works available and select a book to download

 Click the title to view the formats available to the download facility. Download the text to be able to read offline, at any time. It will be saved into the Downloads folder

A Tale of Two Cities by Charles Dickens

Download   **Bibrec**

Read This Book Online

Read this ebook online...

Download This eBook

Format	Size	Mirror Sites		
HTML	897 kB	mirror sites		
EPUB (no images)	318 kB			
Kindle (no images)	1.3 MB			
Plucker	452 kB			
QiOO Mobile	355 kB			
Plain Text UTF-8	774 kB			
More Files...		mirror sites		

There are various mailing lists for Project Gutenberg, to keep you updated when new eBooks are added.

1 Scroll down at http://www.gutenberg.org and select the Mailing lists link

About Us

- About Us: About Project Gutenberg.
- No Cost or Freedom: What does 'free ebook' mean?
- License and Trademark information: What you are allowed to do with the books you download.
- Linking Readme: Information for people who want to link to our site.
- Robot Readme: Information for people who want to robot our site.
- Donate: How to make a donation to Project Gutenberg.
- News and Newsletters: Our news site. Contains the weekly and monthly newsletters by PG Founder Michael Hart (and the newsletter archives).
- How-To's: In depth information about different topics.
- FAQ: Frequently Asked Questions.
- Partners, Affiliates and Resources: A collection of links.
- Credits: Thanks to our most prominent volunteers.
- Mailing lists: Join our mailing lists.
- Contact Information: How to get in touch.

2 Click the links, for example gmonthly, the Project Gutenberg monthly newsletter

Newsletters, with new eBook listings, calls for assistance, general information, and announcements

Project Gutenberg sends a monthly newsletter (there used to be a weekly newsletter, but that has been discontinued):

- gmonthly ☞: Project Gutenberg Monthly newsletter. Traffic consists mostly of one monthly newsletter.

3 Provide an email address – your name is not required. Specify a password, then click Subscribe

gmonthly -- Project Gutenberg Monthly Newsletter

About gmonthly   English (USA)

The monthly newsletter is sent on approximately the first Wednesday of each month. It includes a listing of all new eBooks for the month, as well as some editorial content. The gweekly list is weekly, and includes the same book lists but somewhat more editorial content, announcements, etc.

To see the collection of prior postings to the list, visit the gmonthly Archives.

Using gmonthly

To post a message to all the list members, send email to gmonthly@lists.pglaf.org.

You can subscribe to the list, or change your existing subscription, in the sections below.

Subscribing to gmonthly

Subscribe to gmonthly by filling out the following form.

You will be sent email requesting confirmation, to prevent others from gratuitously subscribing you. This is a hidden list, which means that the list of members is available only to the list administrator.

| Your email address: | |
| Your name (optional): | |

You may enter a privacy password below. This provides only mild security, but should prevent others from messing with your subscription. **Do not use a valuable password** as it will occasionally be emailed back to you in cleartext.

If you choose not to enter a password, one will be automatically generated for you, and it will be sent to you once you've confirmed your subscription. You can always request a mail-back of your password when you edit your personal options.

Pick a password:	
Reenter password to confirm:	
Which language do you prefer to display your messages?	English (USA)
Would you like to receive list mail batched in a daily digest?	● No ○ Yes

Subscribe

4 You'll get an email to confirm your registration

Hot tip

You don't have to provide any personal details to download books, but it is necessary to register if you want updates via email.

Hot tip

As well as listing the latest eBooks, the newsletter contains announcements and calls for assistance. The project is heavily reliant on volunteer help.

Don't forget

You must reply to the email to complete the registration process.

Research Products

Hot tip

As you gain experience and confidence, go on to research product details and prices online, either in preparation for a high street store purchase or simply to increase your awareness.

When you have a purchase in mind, you'll generally go through the same process, whatever the product, and however you ultimately decide to make the purchase:

- Decide what you need
- Establish product prices
- Evaluate the suppliers

If you have just a general idea of the product type, e.g. a digital camera, you need to clarify the requirements and try to reduce your options to a few particular makes and models. Try a website with reviews, advice and buying guides.

1 Visit http://reviews.cnet.com/ and click the Digital Cameras link

Hot tip

The Guide also features a selection of their top cameras.

2 Click the Digital camera buying guide if you are new to digital cameras, to get the specifications explained and to help you decide which features and factors you think are important

Set Preferences

1 Click in the Search field at the top of the window and type "digital camera finder"

Hot tip

Some choices you make may be unavailable in the size range, but you are able to go back and start again.

2 This is a step-by-step guide to help reduce the list to the most suitable models. It covers size, how much manual control you want, and other required features such as image stabilizer

3 With the Results page displayed, tick the check box at the side of several models and then click the Compare Selected button

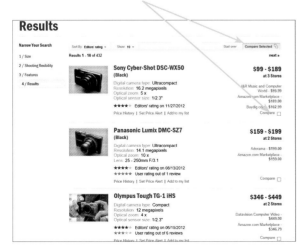

Hot tip

Use the Sort by function to arrange the suitable cameras by Lowest price, Manufacturer or Editor's rating.

4 Prices, ratings and full specifications are provided

Compare Prices

1 The comparison chart gives very full technical details, as well as the editor's and users' ratings

CNET · Reviews · Digital cameras · Sony digital cameras · Compare digital cameras

Digital cameras comparison chart

Product	Sony Cyber-Shot DSC-WX50 (Black)	Panasonic Lumix DMC-SZ7 (Black)	Olympus Tough TG-1 iHS	Sony Cyber-shot DSC-WX50 (Silver)
Price	$99.99 to $189.00	$159.00 to $199.00	$346.79 to $449.00	$94.97 to $119.99
CNET editors' rating	★★★★☆	★★★★☆	★★★★☆	★★★★☆
Average user rating	★★★★★	★★★★★	★★★☆☆	★★★★★
Release date	Info unavailable	Info unavailable	Info unavailable	Info unavailable
Bottom line	The tiny Sony Cyber-shot DSC-WX50 is a lot of camera for the money, with solid shooting performance, and good photo and movie quality	A speedy little camera with a long lens, the Panasonic Lumix DMC-SZ7 performs beyond its tiny price tag.	The Olympus Tough TG-1 iHS combines a bright lens, a high-sensitivity, high-speed sensor, and some nice extras to make it a top rugged compact camera	The tiny Sony Cyber-shot DSC-WX50 is a lot of camera for the money, with solid shooting performance, and good photo and movie quality
Type	LCD display - 2.7 in	TFT active matrix - Color LCD display - 3 in	OLED display - 3 in	LCD display - 2.7 in
Product Type	Digital camera - Compact	Digital camera - Compact	Digital camera - Compact	Digital camera - Compact
Digital zoom	2 x	4 x	4 x	2 x

2 Scroll down to see the list of suppliers of your selected items, the price and availability

Full specifications	Full specifications	Full specifications	Full specifications	Full specifications
Buying choices	J&R Music and Computer World $99.99 In stock: Yes	Adorama $199.00 In stock: Yes	Datavision Computer Video $449.00 In stock: Yes	Adorama $99.00 In stock: Yes
	Amazon.com Marketplace $189.00 In stock: Yes	Amazon.com Marketplace $159.00 In stock: Yes	Amazon.com Marketplace $346.79 In stock: Yes	Buydig.com $99.99 In stock: Yes
	Buydig.com $102.99 In stock: Yes	Prices from 2 stores	Prices from 2 stores	TheNerds.net $119.99 In stock: Yes
	Prices from 3 stores			Prices from 7 stores

3 Select the retailer's name to be transferred to the site if you wish to make a purchase

Type 'comparison shopping' into a search engine such as Google and choose between generic sites that cover all categories of goods, such as PriceGrabber.com or product specific sites such as saveonenergy.com or uSwitch.com in the UK. Many retail outlets such as sears.com also offer the ability to compare products within house.

Register at a Website

When you feel ready to actually buy on the Internet, start with one of the better known websites such as Amazon.

1. Go to http://www.amazon.com and if you haven't already registered, click next to Sign in and select the Start here link to add your details

2. Complete the Registration form with your name, your email address, mobile phone number (optional) and your password. You enter some items twice, so they can be validated

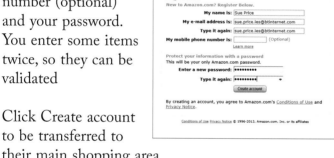

3. Click Create account to be transferred to their main shopping area

4. Search the Amazon website for products that interest you. For example, you could look in the Books section for the latest-prize winning novel

5. Once you have used Amazon, you will find that it remembers items and categories that you have browsed and will list recommended items

117

Buy Online

When you find a product you want to buy, the website guides you through the process, stage by stage:

- Select item and add to shopping cart
- Sign in (if not already signed in)
- Supply delivery address and billing address
- Choose delivery option
- Add gift wrap if required
- Make payment
- Confirm purchase

1 Click Add to Cart to select an item to purchase

2 Click Edit Shopping Cart at any point to review items you have selected

✓ 1 item added to Cart

The Redeemer (A Harry Hole Novel)
by Jo Nesbo
$14.99
☐ This will be a gift

Order subtotal: $14.99
1 item in your Cart

Add $10.01 of eligible items to your order to qualify for **FREE Super Saver Shipping**. (Some restrictions apply)

Edit your Cart | Proceed to checkout

3 When you've chosen all the items you want, click Proceed to Checkout. You will need to be signed in to complete the purchase process

4 Add the delivery address, which may be the same as the billing address, and choose Dispatch to this address

5 Select your delivery option and click or tap Continue

Choose a shipping speed

FREE TWO-DAY SHIPPING FREE Two-Day Shipping on This Order: Try Amazon Prime free for 30 days and get fast, free shipping starting with this order.

● Standard Shipping (3-5 business days)
○ FREE Two-Day Shipping with a free trial of *AmazonPrime* —get it Friday, June 21 (Learn more)
○ Two-Day Shipping —get it Friday, June 21
○ One-Day Shipping —get it tomorrow Thursday, June 20

Buy New $14.99

Quantity: 1 ▾

☐ Yes, I want **FREE Two-Day Shipping** with Amazon Prime

Add to Cart

or

Sign in to turn on 1-Click ordering

Add to Wish List | ▾

6 The process bar at the top of the Amazon page indicates the purchase stage reached

7 If you are sending a gift, click the box for the giftwrap, and complete the message option, gift wrap, etc. Then click Continue to proceed to the Payment stage

8 Select your payment method. For a credit card, enter the type, number, expiry date and the security code

9 Check the order to make sure the details are correct

10 When you are ready, click Place your order

Place your order

Hot tip

You can make any changes you wish, add or remove items, amend shipping and billing addresses, or even cancel the whole order.

Amazon Kindle Books

Using your Amazon account, you can purchase digital versions of books (ebooks) that can be used on both the Kindle reader or on the Kindle app on your Windows PC, tablet or smartphone.

You can share your books on up to six such devices that are registered to that account.

Order Groceries Online

Hot tip

If you're tired of fighting crowds at the grocery store, or if you find the shopping bags too awkward to handle, order your groceries from the comfort of your own home.

1. Type the address of your favorite grocery store in the Explorer window and click the Go button. Or use your usual search engine to identify suitable sites

2. The first step should be to check that the supermarket delivers to your area. Enter your zip code and click Check Zip code

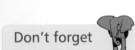

3. Next, register your name, address and other necessary details to create an account, or sign in if you already have an account

4. Use the various tabs to browse the supermarket categories

Don't forget

Click Delivery Info to discover delivery charges, minimum order size and time slots available in your area.

5. For example, click the What's Good tab to see special deals, promotions and new products

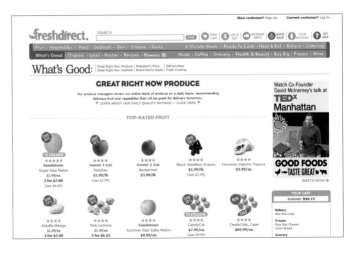

6 Choose a tab such as Grocery and the list will be extended into subcategories. Click a particular item, such as Cereals, for a full list from which to select

7 As you add items, the contents of your cart are displayed on the right, with a running total of your spending

8 Select View Cart to review your list and to increase quantities or remove items. Click Update quantities to ensure that any changes are recognized

9 Select Checkout when finished and supply credit card details to complete the purchase

Buying and Selling on eBay

The eBay website is an online marketplace where anyone can trade products. It started life like an electronic flea market, but now it is also used by large commercial retailers too. The eBay sellers pay a listing fee, plus a percentage if the items sell. Private and commercial sellers are subject to differing rates. eBay buyers visit and use the marketplace without any surcharges. What makes it safe and workable is that any parties that abuse the system will be disciplined or ejected.

There are differences from a regular flea market:

- The eBay marketplace is international
- There is a huge choice of goods
- Sales can be auction or fixed price format
- Buyers don't see the product in person before the sale

Buying sight-unseen is quite a challenge, but buyers and sellers can have some trust in the website because of the feedback mechanism that rates the quality of sales and purchase experiences.

To get started on eBay, click the Customer Support link to access the eBay Learning Center, with help on buying and selling.

eBay provides its own Buyer Protection to help give you confidence in its processes.

 Type "Buyer Protection" into the search field and click the link for details of how problems are resolved

Hot tip

eBay Buyer Protection covers you when an item is not as described or does not arrive. It lists exceptions such as vehicles, real estate and business equipment categories. It does cover purchases made with PayPal and many other electronic payment methods.

123

PayPal

PayPal is the payment scheme owned by eBay, that you can use to pay for your purchases. You will need to open an account with them, when you buy or when you sell items. It stores and protects your financial information and deals with third parties on your behalf. Visit www.paypal.com and select the link to Security at the bottom of the page.

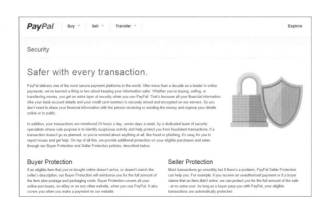

Internet Fraud Prevention

Keep the following tips in mind to help ensure that your online shopping experience is a safe one:

1. Look for accurate, clear and easily-accessible information about the goods or services being offered, and clarify any queries before you place an order

2. Understand the terms and conditions, and get a full, itemized list of costs involved, including currency conversions and delivery charges

3. Verify the seller's name, city, email ID and phone number, all of which should be easily available from the seller

4. If the price is very low compared to the retail value, take extra steps to verify the seller's claims. Remember, if it's too good to be true, there's probably a catch

 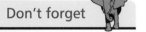
5. Request proof of ownership when buying from private parties. For example, for a vehicle, they should produce evidence of title, registration and vehicle identification number

6. Request proof of possession. Request information or photos that only someone in possession of the items could supply, for example a close-up view of a specific part

7. Be cautious with international sellers. If a dispute arises in the transaction, your home country laws may not apply to the international seller

8. Use credit cards or debit cards for payments, since wire transfer services do not always provide protection or refunds

7 Letters and Reports

Create many types of documents – letters, notes and reports. Apply fancy fonts and formats to add interest to your work. Learn useful techniques, such as copy and paste and creating templates, to save you time and effort.

Working on the Desktop

The apps which have been described so far all operate from the Start screen, and occupy the whole screen to take full advantage of the computer's screen size.

The Microsoft Office programs – Word, Excel, Powerpoint, OneNote and Outlook – although they open from the Start screen, work in the Desktop environment. These programs open in windows which can be resized, minimized and moved. Their status – open or closed – is indicated by their icons on the Taskbar at the bottom of the screen. To see this in action:

1. Tap the tile to open the Desktop and click the Explorer button

2. Click the Resize button on the Title bar to switch between full screen or window

Minimise   Resize

Close

3. Select the Minimize button to hide the window, or the Explorer button to restore

4. Drag an edge with mouse or finger to stretch the window, or select the Title bar to move it

5. Click the Taskbar application icon to switch between open files within a program as shown or between open windows (Word and Explorer)

A Simple Document

In this section we will be creating a simple document using the word processor, Microsoft Word. It is supplied with the Surface RT tablet or is available as part of the Microsoft Office suite of programs.

With a word processor you can create a document, move and copy text, insert or remove words or whole paragraphs, change the layout and add images. It provides facilities such as a spelling and grammar checker and thesaurus.

You can save the document to disk and then retrieve it later, make a few changes and use it again, without needing to retype the whole document. You can print one or several copies at a time.

Microsoft Word is a WYSIWYG (what you see is what you get) system, meaning that the final document will print exactly as you see it on the screen.

1 From the Start screen, swipe or scroll to the Word tile and tap to open the program

2 The program opens with a list of available document templates, the first of which is a blank document. Tap to select it

3 On the blank page (with the name Document 1 in the title bar), the cursor or printing point will appear as a flashing vertical bar near the top left of the window. This is the start of the typing area as the space above and to the left of the cursor is the default or standard margin allowance

Hot tip

Start your word processing practice with a few simple tasks, such as notes or draft documents.

Hot tip

The first time you open an Office document you will be required to select a file format. See page 130.

Hot tip

Default is a word often used in computing. It simply means "as standard". For example in the US, Letter size paper is the default, in the UK it is A4.

...cont'd

The Word Document Window

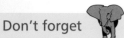
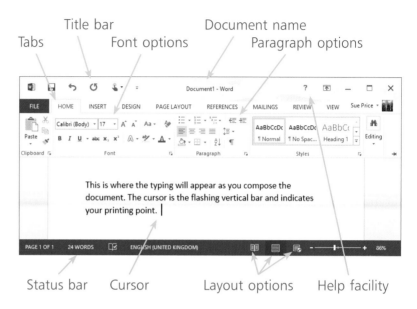

Tabs | Title bar | Document name
Font options | Paragraph options

Status bar | Cursor | Layout options | Help facility

1. Type a few lines of text. You don't need to press Enter or Carriage Return at the end of the line of text, as was necessary with a typewriter. The text will flow automatically on to the next line. This is known as text wrap

2. When you have typed a few lines of text and need to start a new paragraph, press the Enter key twice. The first press starts a new line, and the second gives you a blank line between paragraphs

3. Red wavy lines underneath text indicate a spelling mistake. Green lines indicate incorrect grammar

4. If you type more than a screenful of text, swipe up, or use the scroll bars at the side of the window to move up and down. If you have a wheel on your mouse you can use that instead

Save the Document

1 Click File and Save or alternatively click or tap the disk button on the Quick access toolbar

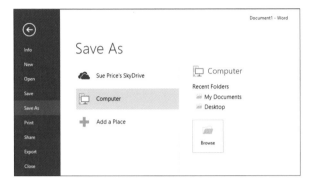

2 Select Computer, then My Documents to save it to your hard drive

3 Word uses the first line of the document as the file name. If this is not suitable, just type a new name. Any text highlighted in blue will be overwritten

4 Click Save. The document is saved into the Documents library. Thereafter, you will only need to click on the disk button to update the file

Hot tip

If this is the first time you have saved the file, it will open the Save As window.

Hot tip

When you name and save a file, the title bar shows the new name instead of Document One.

...cont'd

Save With a New Name

Use Save As to save a file with a different name from the original. In this way you can create a second or different version of the file without having to retype the whole document.

1 Click File and Save As. Click in the File name field and change the name, then click Save

Save As a New File Type

Word 2013 (and Word 2010) documents have the file extension .docx added to identify them to the operating system. Older Word programs, such as Word 2003 used the file extension .doc. The newer versions of Word can open older documents, but the opposite is not true. Word 2003 cannot open .docx files. To save a file to be readable in the older programs:

1 Select File, Save As and click the arrow on Save as type

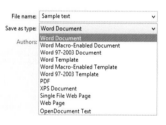

2 Choose Word 97-2003 document, or alternatively .PDF to be readable by almost all computers

Microsoft Office Default File Types

The first time you open any of the Office programs you have the choice of which file type to use. The better choice is Office Open XML Formats. To select this option later:

1 Open Word and choose File, Options, Save and choose Word document (*.docx)

File Management

The hard disk (C: drive) inside your PC is like a very large filing cabinet. It provides permanent storage for all the programs and system files required to run the computer and all the data files that you create – documents, spreadsheets, photos, etc.

The files on your computer are organized by User, into folders and Libraries (groups of related folders). To view the organization:

 Open the Desktop and click the File Explorer icon on the Taskbar

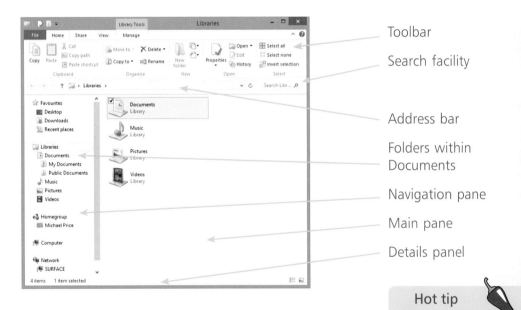

Toolbar

Search facility

Address bar

Folders within Documents

Navigation pane

Main pane

Details panel

131

 The Navigation pane on the left shows the Library and the related folders grouped within it, for example My Documents and Public Documents

 Click on the ▷ sign next to a folder to expand it and display any subfolders. Click on ◢ to contract the folder

- ▲ ♪ Music
  - ▷ 🎵 My Music
  - ▷ 🎵 Public Music
- ▷ 🖼 Pictures
- ▷ 🎬 Videos

Hot tip

Think of the folders as drawers within a filing cabinet. Folders can contain both subfolders and files.

Hot tip

Double-click or double-tap a folder in the main pane to open it to view the contents. If you have trouble with the double-click process, click once and press Enter.

View Documents Library

All the data files that you create are stored by default in the Documents Library. As we have seen previously, images will be stored in the Pictures folder, and music in the Music folder, but the parent folder is always the User's folder. If you have more than one user on the PC (see page 212) each can have their own User name and folders.

1. In File Explorer, select Documents to view the contents of the Documents library. This view shows files in both My Documents and Public Documents

2. Click My Documents to view only those files contained within this folder

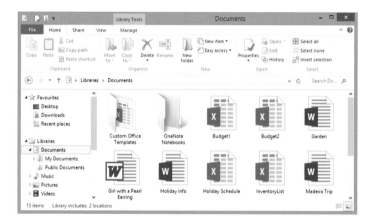

3. Click the Views button to change the way files are displayed. Select Details to see the file size and date created

4. Each file displayed has an icon indicating which software it is associated with. Open any file from this window by double-clicking on the file icon

Organize Your Documents

As the number of files increases, it's a good idea to create new folders, so that you don't have to scroll through numerous files to find the one you want.

1 Open Documents, select the Home tab and click or tap New Folder on the toolbar

2 The new folder will appear with New Folder highlighted in blue. Type in the required name and press Enter

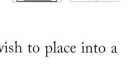

For existing files in Documents that you wish to place into a subfolder:

1 Select the file, and drag it towards the folder. When the folder turns blue, release the mouse button

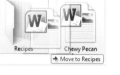

2 As an alternative, select the file, and on the Home tab, click Cut. Double-click or double tap on the folder to open it and select Paste

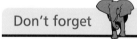

You can create new folders within the Office programs as you save your files. For example, in Word:

1 With your document open, select File, Save As and in the window click the New Folder button. Name the folder then double-click on it to open it. Click Save to save the file into the new folder

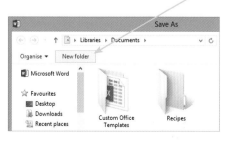

Hot tip

If you click away from the New Folder name, it will automatically be called New Folder. Right-click the icon and select Rename from the menu.

Don't forget

If you are not comfortable with using the mouse to drag files, using Cut and Paste is a safer way to move files into folders.

133

Retrieve Your Document

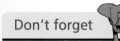

Don't forget

You can open any document by going to the Desktop, opening the required folder and double clicking/ tapping the file.

Don't forget

Each Windows program is designed to look for only its own files and filter out other programs' files. So when you open the word processor, you only see files that can be opened with the word processor. When you open the Documents Library from the Start menu, you see all file types.

1 Open Word and recently created/ edited documents will be listed. Simply click to select

2 For older or unlisted files select Open Other Documents. Click Computer, and then My Documents

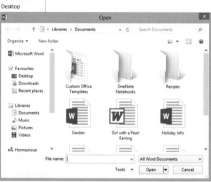

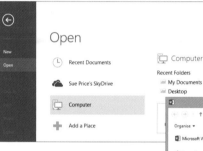

3 To locate your file, you may need to scroll down or across the window. If it's in a subfolder, double-click on the subfolder to open it and double-click on the file icon

Finding Files

At any time use the Charms bar Search function to locate a file. Select Files and type the file name in the Search box.

Edit Your Document

Insert Text

Word processors have two typing modes, insert and overtype. The keyboard is set to insert when you open the program, so all you need to do is to take the cursor to where you want the word and start typing. Any text to the right will be pushed along and if necessary will wrap to the next line.

Pressing the Insert key on the keyboard (often done accidentally) switches to overtype mode, and any words you type will replace the existing text.

Delete Text

For small amounts of text, or individual letters, use the Delete and Backspace keyboard keys. Backspace deletes text to the left and above the cursor, Delete removes text to the right and below.

The Undo and Redo Feature

As you work, most programs keep a running log of your actions. This means that you can actually step backwards and undo some of  the changes you have made, for example deleting text. Once you have used Undo, you can then Redo if you change your mind yet again. The log of your actions will usually be maintained until you close the program, although some programs only remember a few steps. Note, however, that you cannot undo a Save.

The Spell Checker

1. Select the Review tab from the Office ribbon. Click the Spell check button. It will step through the document. Click Change to accept a suggestion, or Ignore

2. Select Add to add the word to your dictionary. This is useful for items such as place names which may not be recognized

Hot tip

To insert a blank line at the very top of the document, take the cursor to the top, left margin and press the Enter key.

Hot tip

Delete and Backspace keys remove blank lines or part blank lines. With the cursor at the left margin press Delete to remove blank lines below or press Backspace to remove blank lines above.

Beware

Select Change for an individual mis-spelled word. If there is a word you wish to change throughout the document, check the results on a few first. Change all can have unintended consequences.

Print Your Document

1 Click File > Print to access printing options

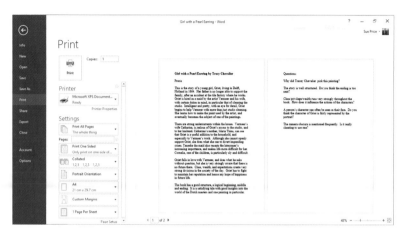

2 The right-hand pane gives a preview of the printed document. Use the percentage slider to view it in greater detail. Use the forward and back arrows to scroll through the document

3 Print all pages is the default action. Specify ranges or individual pages in the Pages field. Type page numbers separated by a comma (e.g. 1,3,7) or ranges separated with a hyphen (e.g. 3-6)

4 Click the Print all pages button to display further options

5 Select which printer to use, if you have more than one available, and to print double-sided if you have this option on your printer

6 Specify the number of copies and then click the large Print button

---

Hot tip

Click the down arrow on the right of the Quick Access toolbar to add the Quick print button. Note that using this button will print the whole document.

Customize Quick Access Toolbar

New

Open

✓ Save

Quick Print

Don't forget

Paper size, orientation and margins will normally be set within the document on the Page Layout tab.

Working with Text

The easiest way to work with most documents is to first create them and then apply any formatting, font and alignment (positioning) changes. To do this you need to select the text first. There are several ways to do this:

 To select a whole line, such as a title, position the mouse arrow in the left margin, so it is pointing at the text. Then click with the left mouse button

Hot tip

Word opens with a default style with presets for font size, type, alignment and spacing.

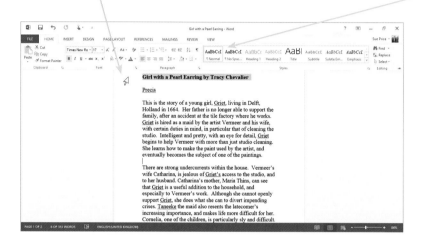

Use the same method for several lines or a whole paragraph, but this time click and hold the mouse button as you drag down the page

For text in the middle of a paragraph, click with the mouse at the beginning of the required text, hold down the Shift key and click at the end

Use the cursor (arrow) keys if you find the mouse difficult. Position the cursor at the beginning of the text, press and hold the Shift key and use any of the arrow keys

Remove the highlight by clicking outside the highlighted area

Beware

If you press the Enter key or the Tab key when text is highlighted it will be deleted. Click the Undo button to get it back.

Hot tip

Double-click on a single word to select it. Press Ctrl + A to select the whole document.

Move and Copy

Type it once and use it many times! Once you have entered some information into your PC, you can move it around or copy it from one place to another, and even copy it from one file to another. To move text:

1. Select the text using one of the methods described on the previous page

2. On the Home tab, click on the Cut button. The text will disappear from view

3. Position the cursor where you wish to place the text

4. Click on the Paste button. Alternatively, click on the arrow under the Paste icon to select Paste Options which relate to text formatting

To copy text:

1. Select the text as before

2. Select the Copy button. This time the text stays in place, but an exact copy is placed into the computer's memory

3. Position the cursor where you wish to repeat the text and select Paste

The Clipboard

Word allows you to hold up to 24 different items in the Clipboard. Click the arrow in the corner of the Clipboard section to see text or images you have cut or copied. You can then choose which to paste.

Enhance Your Document

There are many ways to make your document look more interesting, or to emphasize particular words or sections.

1 Use bold, italic or underline for titles or individual words. Select the text (see page 137) and then click on any or all of the buttons. They act as toggle switches; first click turns them on, second turns them off

B **I** **U** ▾

(see page 137)

Hot tip

Use the Change case button to swiftly change existing text to uppercase, sentence case or to toggle case.

2 Select a different font for part or all of the document. Again, select your text first then click the down arrow next to the Font style field to view the available fonts, displayed as they will appear in the document

Times New Roman

- 𝑂 BatangChe
- 𝑂 Book Antiqua
- 𝑂 Bookman Old Style
- 𝑂 Bookshelf Symbol 7
- 𝑂 Bradley Hand ITC
- 𝑂 Browallia New
- 𝑂 BrowalliaUPC

Aa ▾

- <u>S</u>entence case.
- <u>l</u>owercase
- <u>U</u>PPERCASE
- <u>C</u>apitalize Each Word
- t<u>OGGLE</u> c<u>ASE</u>

3 Using other options on the Font section of the ribbon, you can change the font size, color, create subscript, superscript and strike-through text. Use the Format eraser to remove all formatting

17 ▾ A˄ A˅ Aa ▾

abc x₂ x² A ▾ ab ▾ A ▾

Font

4 Highlight a line or paragraph of text and click on the Increase Indent button one or more times to indent the text

Old Lang Syne

by Robert Burns

Should old acquaintance be forgot,
And never brought to mind?
Should auld acquaintance be forgot,
And old lang syne?

    For old lang syne, my dear,
    For old lang syne,
    We'll tak a cup o' kindness yet,
    For old lang syne.

And surely ye'll be your pint-stowp,
And surely I'll be mine!

Hot tip

Press the Tab key one or more times to indent a line of text.

Write a Letter

When you start any word processing task, the text is always aligned to the left margin (Align Left). This is the standard presentation format. Titles will often be centered on the paper and in some documents, for example books, text is straight on both left and right margins. This is known as justified text.

Word processors provide you with tools to align your text, so that the text will stay centered, aligned or justified, even if you change the size of the paper or the margins:

Align Left — Center — Align Right — Justify

Whether you are writing a formal or an informal letter, both will start with your address at the top, either centered or aligned to the right of the paper. To enter your address and position it on the paper:

1 Type your address on the left and select or highlight the whole address. Then click on the Align Right button

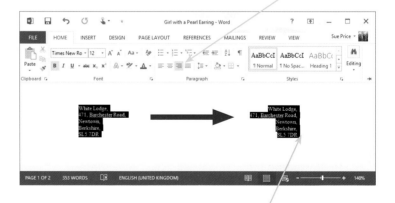

2 Click with the mouse to the right of the last line of the address and press Enter. This clears the highlight, but the cursor will remain at the right margin

3 Click the Align Left button to return to the left margin to continue the letter

Address the Envelope

1 Highlight the recipient's address, click the Mailings tab and Envelopes

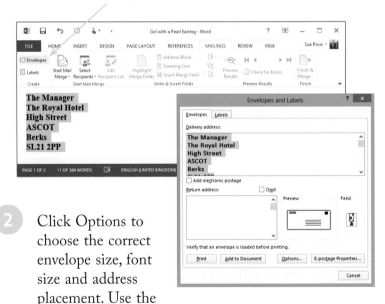

2 Click Options to choose the correct envelope size, font size and address placement. Use the preview window to check the result

3 When ready, click the Print button

Create a Template

Hot tip

Using a template saves much time and effort. Microsoft provides many templates with all its Office programs. To view those available in Word, select the File tab and New.

It used to be normal to buy pre-printed letterhead stationery, but with a computer you can actually make your own. You can design a layout for your address, apply color, font styles, and even add a picture and save the letterhead as a template. You can then use the template whenever you wish.

1   Open Word and you are presented with a wide array of templates from which to choose. Select Blank document

2   In the new document, type in the details of your address. Position the text, centered or right aligned and apply any font enhancements

3   To add an automatic date field to the letterhead, select the Insert tab from the ribbon

Beware

The date field is updated when you open the document. You will need to look in the Documents folder at the file details if you want to check the original date of the document.

4   Position the cursor where you want the date to appear, and click the Date & Time button

5 Select a format for the date and make sure to tick Automatically update when printed. Click OK to finish

6 Enter any other details you would like to see in your template

7 Select File > Save As and beneath the file name field click the down arrow for other document types. Select Word Template. Name the file as usual and select Save

8 The next time you open Word or select New, your template will be available within a new category – Personal

9 Click the Pin to have the template permanently available

10 You can also Pin it to the list of Recent documents

Hot tip

The template is saved into Custom Office Templates, a hidden folder.

Hot tip

Select Take a tour in the list of templates for some tips and tricks within Word.

Create a Table

1 With the cursor at the point you wish to start the table, click the Insert tab on the ribbon

2 Click the Table button and drag the mouse to the right and down, selecting the number of columns and rows required. Then, release the mouse button

● Text will automatically wrap within a cell and the cell will expand to accommodate it

> Text will automatically wrap within a cell, all you have to do is type

● Use the Tab key to move from cell to cell

● Columns can be narrowed or widened as required. Position the cursor on a column divider and drag the line in either direction

● With the cursor inside the table area the Design and Layout tabs become available. Use the Design tab for color, shading, borders and style. Use the Layout tab to add columns and rows and for positioning within cells

January	February	March	April	May	June

8 Money Management

Set up a household budget to manage your personal finances. Create and track a share portfolio, using the Internet to get up-to-date prices and details, with the PC doing all the record keeping and calculations.

Household Budget

Microsoft Excel is the spreadsheet program in the Office suite. It lets you create lists and calculate values, using formulas where required. You can input figures, change the figures, and the spreadsheet will recalculate the changes automatically. To see how this works we will create something that we all need, a household budget.

To open the spreadsheet:

Don't forget

A spreadsheet is the computerized version of the original ledger sheet.

1   On the Start screen, swipe or scroll sideways and click or tap Microsoft Excel

2   The format is the same as that of Word. You are presented with a list of Recent workbooks (none in the first instance) and a variety of templates. Select Blank workbook

Hot tip

On the first time of opening, you may be asked to select file types for Excel to open. Just click No as the default files types (the ones already pre-defined) are the ones you want.

3   An empty spreadsheet is displayed, showing the column labels (A, B, C...) and the row numbers (1, 2, 3...) used to identify the spaces or cells in the spreadsheet

Don't forget

In the spreadsheet the cursor position is indicated by a green outline around the current cell.

4   The location of the current cell is shown in the Address bar, under the File tab. This location, for example, is cell C5. This is referred to as its cell reference or address. Later in the chapter we learn how to use the cell reference in calculations

Add Headings

① Click cell A1, type the heading Household Budget and press Enter

② In cell A2, type the heading Income and press Enter

③ Press the Tab key, so the cursor moves to cell B3 and type the heading Budget. Press Tab again, and type Actual in C3. Press Tab, and type Over/Under in D3. Press Tab, and type Notes in E3

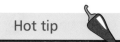

Add Data Rows

① Click cell A4, type Pension and press Enter, to go to the cell below

② Type Salary in A5, and press Enter. Type Bank Interest in A6, and type Share Dividend in A7, pressing Enter after each

③ In the cell below the last Income item, type the label Total Income and press Enter

④ Click the Disk (Save) on the Quick Access toolbar and type a file name such as Budget. Click the Save button to store the spreadsheet file on the hard disk

Show Expenses and Values

Add some values to complete this section of the spreadsheet. Just put typical amounts at this stage.

1 Click in the cell below the Budget heading, and type an amount for the income type, pressing Enter after each entry

	A	B	C	D	E
C8				*fx*	
1	Household Budget				
2	Income				
3		Budget	Actual	Over/Under	Notes
4	Pension	2500	2560		
5	Salary	500	456.75		
6	Bank inter	100	150		
7	Share divi	75	65		
8	Total Income				
9					

2 Click below Actual, and type amounts for the income types, pressing Enter after each. Make some higher and some lower than the budgeted amounts

3 Move the mouse pointer over the line separating the column names (e.g. between A and B). When the pointer turns to the double arrow, click and drag the column divider (or double-click) to fit to the widest entry

	A	B	C
C8			*fx*
1	Household Budget		
2	Income		
3		Budget	Actual
4	Pension	2500	2560
5	Salary	500	456.75
6	Bank interest	100	150
7	Share dividend	75	65
8	Total Income		

4 Add an Expenses section below the Income section, with the same headings as for Income, and a label in column A for each expense type

5 Below the expenses add Total Expenses and Net Income labels

A10	fx	Expenses			
	A	B	C	D	E
10	Expenses	Budget	Actual	Over/Under	Notes
11	Tax	500.00	510.00		
12	Medical	275.00	285.00		
13	House Insurance	50.00	60.00		
14	Car Insurance	30.00	40.00		
15	Cable TV	30.00	30.00		
16	Telephone	20.00	25.00		
17	Mobile cellphone	30.00	35.00		
18	Water	35.00	35.00		
19	Electricity	45.00	45.00		
20	Groceries	600.00	550.00		
21	Vacation	300.00	200.00		
22	Travel	100.00	150.00		
23	Total Expenses				
24	Net Income				

Autosum

Now, insert the formulas to total the Actual Income, Budget Expenses and Actual Expenses. The Autosum command on the ribbon is the simplest way to do this.

1 Select the cell below the amounts and click Autosum on the toolbar. Press Enter or the tick on the Formula bar to accept the formula

AutoSum

Autosum will select the range of numbers adjacent to the results cell. These could be above or to the side, depending on the spreadsheet layout.

Simple Calculations

While the Autosum tool provides a quick and simple way to add columns and rows, there are many times when all you need is a very simple operation. For example, to calculate the difference between the Actual and the Budget amounts:

1 Click in the cell below Over/Under (D4) and type = Click Actual amount (C4), and type - (minus) Click Budget amount (B4) and press Enter

2 Note that the Formula bar shows the actual formula that is in the cell. The result of the calculation is displayed in the cell itself

> **Beware**
>
> Always check the range that Autosum offers. Autosum will add figures to the side if there are no numbers or just one number above the target cell.

149

> **Don't forget**
>
> All formulas begin with an = sign.
>
> The operators are:
>
> + Plus
> - Minus
> * Multiply
> / Divide

Calculations

Excel provides several ways to perform calculations in the spreadsheet. We have used the Autosum function and also simple formulas on the previous page. These are straightforward calculations. Excel, however, is capable of very complex calculations. To understand and use more complicated formulas we will use the Insert Function tool.

Insert Function

1 Click the Insert Function button on the Formula bar to open the Insert Function dialog box

2 You can type a question to search for a formula or click the down arrow to see the 12 categories of function

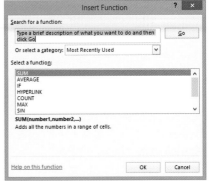

3 We will select a simple formula such as Average and use a mileage list as illustrated

4 With Average selected from the list Click OK. This opens the Function Arguments window

Monthly Mileage	
Jan	2552
Feb	3256
Mar	4895
Apr	3636
May	1254
Jun	7562
Jul	5450
Aug	4568
Sep	6389
Average	=

5 The window, displayed on the next page describes the formula and indicates which data it is using to perform the Average calculation

The Function Arguments dialog window describes the action of the formula and gives a preview of the result.

6 In the Number 1 field, the Function displays the address of the data above the current cursor position. If this is acceptable, click OK

7 To select a different range of cells, click the Collapse dialog box and use the mouse to select the new data range

8 Then use the Expand dialog box to restore the Function Arguments window and click OK

Excel follows standard mathematical precedence. For example $=7+2*3$ returns 13, not 27. Multiplication and division before addition and subtraction.

9 The result is shown in the selected cell

Help with Functions

Within the Insert Function dialog window Excel provides two levels of assistance. Click the question mark on the Insert Function title bar for generic help with formulas, or click the link Help on this function at the bottom left of the window for specific information on the formula syntax and construction.

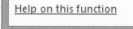

Copy and Paste

To complete the spreadsheet you can use the copy command.

1 Select the subtraction (D4) and right-click. Select Copy from the menu. Drag down to cover the remaining Over/Under cells, right-click and then Paste from the menu

2 Repeat this for the Expenses Over/Under cells

3 This copies the formula and pastes it into the other cells, automatically adjusting cell references

Paste Options

1 The norm when copying formula as shown above is to paste the same formula with adjusted cell references

2 Other options are shown, under Paste Options, and by Paste Special. Hover the mouse over each icon to get the screen tip and preview for the action of each

3 The Paste Special menu item at the very bottom enables even greater control over the paste action

152

The Fill Tool

The Fill tool can also be used to copy formulas. The Fill option is found on the Home tab, but can be more easily used by positioning the mouse on the bottom right corner of the active cell. The mouse symbol changes to the Fill handle, a black +.

1 To fill a range of cells with the same formula, select the starting cell and get the Fill handle. Press the left mouse button and drag to cover the required cells

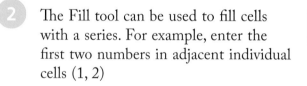

Actual	Over/Under
2,550.00	50.00
455.75	
150.00	
65.00	

Actual	Over/Under
2,550.00	50.00
455.75	-44.25
150.00	0.00
65.00	-10.00

Hot tip

Excel also features autocomplete to fill cells with matching labels. Just press Enter to accept the suggestion or continue typing to ignore.

Charles Dickens
William Shakespeare
Charles Dickens

2 The Fill tool can be used to fill cells with a series. For example, enter the first two numbers in adjacent individual cells (1, 2)

1
2

3 Highlight both cells and select the Fill handle from the bottom cell. Drag to fill the required range

1
2
3
4
5
6

4 Use the Fill tool for swift entering of standard data such as days of the week, months and years

	A	B	C	D
1	Monday			
2				
3			Wednesday	

5 Try different patterns such as 0, 5, 10 or dates for example 01/01/2014

01/01/2014
02/01/2014
03/01/2014
04/01/2014
05/01/2014
06/01/2014

...cont'd

6 Use Fill Series on the Home tab to complete larger amounts such as 1-250 and choose between rows or columns for the entries

Series		
Series in	**Type**	**Date unit**
● Rows	● Linear	● Day
○ Columns	○ Growth	○ Weekday
	○ Date	○ Month
	○ AutoFill	○ Year

☐ Trend

Step value: 1   Stop value: [ ]

OK   Cancel

7 To create your own custom list, first enter the names or items into the spreadsheet as a list. Click the File tab and Options, then Advanced. Scroll down to Edit Custom Lists where you will be able to import it for future use

Relative and Absolute Cell References

The spreadsheet uses relative cell references in its formulas, for example the formula shown here is subtracting B2 from C2 and putting the answer in D2.

Budget	Actual	Over/Under
2500	2550	=C4-B4
500	455.75	=C5-B5
150	150	=C6-B6
75	65	=C7-B7

It is subtracting the cell 2 to the left from the cell 1 to the left of the formula. When you fill a range with the Fill tool, Excel uses the relative position of the formula to the data and adjusts the calculation accordingly.

There are occasions when you need to calculate by a standard amount, for example state tax or VAT. Then you will need

	A	B	C	D	E
1	ITEM	PRICE	QUANTITY	TOTAL	SALES TAX
2	Tyres	39.99	5	=C2*B2	=D2*B7
3	Chains	24.5	8	=C3*B3	=D3*B7
4	Pedals	9.99	24	=C4*B4	=D4*B7
5	Gears	58.75	10	=C5*B5	=D5*B7
6					
7	Sales Tax	0.85			

to reference a particular cell all the time. This is a fixed or Absolute cell reference. The $ symbol is used to fix the column and row in this example, D7 but you can also have a mixed reference where only the row or column is fixed, such as $B7 or B$7.

Hot tip

You can create formulas using just numbers, but by using cell references, e.g. =Sum(A4:A8) or =B2+B3 in your formulas, any changes you make to the data are immediately reflected in the result of the formulas, as the spreadsheet automatically recalculates the data.

Apply Formatting

1 Select the title and the adjacent cells, click Merge and Center

2 Select headers and labels and change font sizes and styles

3 Select cells with amounts, and choose a display format. Click the individual options or the arrow next to General for a list of formats

	A	B	C	D	E
1		Household Budget			
2	**Income**				
3		Budget	Actual	Over/Under	Notes
4	Pension	2,500.00	2,550.00	50.00	
5	Salary	500.00	455.75	-44.25	
6	Bank Interest	150.00	150.00	0.00	
7	Share Dividend	75.00	65.00	-10.00	
8	Total Income	3,225.00	3,220.75	-4.25	
9	**Expenses**				
10		Budget	Actual	Over/Under	Notes
11	Tax	500.00	510.00	10.00	
12	Medical	275.00	285.00	10.00	
13	House Insurance	50.00	60.00	10.00	paid annually
14	Car Insurance	30.00	40.00	10.00	
15	Cable TV	30.00	30.00	0.00	
16	Telephone	20.00	25.00	5.00	
17	Mobile cellphone	30.00	35.00	5.00	
18	Water	35.00	35.00	0.00	
19	Electricity	45.00	45.00	0.00	
20	Groceries	600.00	550.00	-50.00	
21	Vacation	300.00	200.00	-100.00	
22	Travel	100.00	150.00	50.00	
23	Total Expenses	2,015.00	1,965.00	-50.00	
24	**Net Income**				
25					

General ▾

🔳 ▾ % , ←.0 .00 .00 →.0

Number 🔲

Format Cells ? ✕

Number | Alignment | Font | Border | Fill | Protection

Category:
General
Number
Currency
Accounting
Date
Time
Percentage
Fraction
Scientific
Text
Special
Custom

Sample
  Net Income

Decimal places: 2 ⬍

☐ Use 1000 Separator (,)

Negative numbers:
-1234.10
1234.10
-1234.10
-1234.10

Number is used for general display of numbers. Currency and Accounting offer specialized formatting for monetary value.

OK   Cancel

4 Click the small arrow in the corner of the Number section for more control over number display

5 Select the row of cells at a main heading such as Income or Expenses, and choose a Fill color

6 Alternatively, use the Styles section on the Home tab to apply consistent heading styles, colors and formats to the spreadsheet

Good, Bad and Neutral					
Normal	Bad	Good	Neutral		
Data and Model					
Calculation	Check Cell	Explanatory ...	Input	Linked Cell	Note
Output	Warning Text				

Hot tip

Add various formatting to the spreadsheet to make it easier to view important items.

Don't forget

You can specify the number of decimal places, show negative values in red and add separators to the 1000s values.

Control the View

Freeze Panes

When the spreadsheet gets too big to view the contents on the monitor without scrolling, you may need to keep the headings and row labels in view.

1 Click the View tab and Freeze panes. Select your preferred option from the list shown

2 To retain more than just the first column or row, position the cursor to the right of the row labels, and below the headings you wish to keep in view. Then select Freeze panes

3 Click Unfreeze panes when finished

View Two Spreadsheets Simultaneously

You can copy and paste between spreadsheets, or work with two or more at a time.

1 Open both spreadsheets, click the View tab and View Side by Side

2 Click Arrange All to choose whether horizontally, vertically, etc.

Check Formulas

Excel provides Formula auditing tools to help prevent errors occurring in your spreadsheet. The simplest example is when you get a comment such as #Value! or #Num! in a cell, indicating that the formula is not valid. You are then offered help with the formula.

Hot tip

When a cell shows ###### it is not an error but an overflow. Just widen the column to reveal the actual contents.

Another notification is a mark in the corner of a cell indicating inconsistent formula.

To view formulas on the spreadsheet:

 Click the Formulas tab, then Show Formulas

Don't forget

When you insert a column or row you may need to update the formula to include the new data.

157

2. Select a cell with a formula and click the option to Trace Precedents and Trace Dependents. Arrows appear on the spreadsheet indicating the underlying data. Select Remove arrows to clear

Hot tip

To show formulas quickly, press Ctrl + ` (the key above the tab key). Press again to return to values.

3. Click Error Checking to validate formulas on the whole spreadsheet

Error Checking

Error in cell D5

=C5-B5+6

Inconsistent Formula

The formula in this cell differs from the formulas in this area of the spreadsheet.

Copy Formula from Above

Help on this error

Ignore Error

Edit in Formula Bar

Options...   Previous   Next

Print the Spreadsheet

The spreadsheet has the potential to be a huge document. As noted on the previous page, it has over 16,000,000,000 cells. When its time to print, you have to specify what and how.

1 Click the View tab and change from Normal view to Page Layout view to get an immediate indication of how the document will print

2 Click the Page Layout tab to adjust margins, orientation and paper size

Hot tip

Use Page Break View to adjust the page break positioning.

Hot tip

The Header/Footer design tools are directly available on the Insert tab.

3 Click where indicated to add a Header, or alternatively, scroll down to add to the Footer area

4 With the Header or Footer area selected, click the new Design tab that appears to add specific items to the Header/Footer area. Click the button to switch between Header and Footer

5 Click the Print Titles button to open the Page Setup window. From here, you can select which rows and columns to repeat when the spreadsheet flows on to a second or more pages

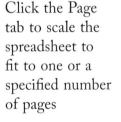

6 Click the Minimize window to select the rows and Maximize to restore

7 Tick the box to Print Gridlines if required. Click Row and column headings to have A,B,C and 1,2,3 print as well. This is particularly useful if you are printing with formulas showing

8 Click the Page tab to scale the spreadsheet to fit to one or a specified number of pages

9 You can print just an area of the spreadsheet. Select using the Page Setup window above, or preselect the area and go straight to the Print menu. Click the arrow on Print Active Sheets to view the options

Beware

Merged cells, used to display the main spreadsheet title, interfere with selecting columns to display on every page.

Hot tip

As an alternative to printing gridlines, use the Borders option on the Home tab to outline specific areas of the sheet.

Don't forget

All these page setup elements are available on the Print menu where you will also get a full preview of the print layout.

159

Track Your Stock Portfolio

1. Open a blank spreadsheet and enter details of your stocks and shares. You could enter, for example, the quantity, and record the price periodically, so you can review the changes

	A	B	C	D	E	F	G
1				Stock Portfolio			
2	Company	Dell	IBM	Microsoft	Rolls Royce	Shell	Foster's
3	Currency	us$1	us$1	us$1	£0.01	£0.01	aus$1
4	Quantity	10	5	20	8	4	50
5	Symbol	DELL	IBM	MSFT	RR	SHEL	FGL
6	01/01/2009	38.44	108.49	43.26	175.21	391.65	3.60
7	01/01/2010	26.12	108.75	26.99	167.68	499.32	4.12
8	01/01/2011	27.49	105.28	28.16	134.24	429.92	4.41
9	01/01/2012	23.86	76.87	20.98	86.77	337.44	4.06
10	01/01/2013	33.44	98.28	24.66	175.47	347.98	4.15
11	01/01/2014	41.76	93.24	26.2	261.12	463.50	5.21
12	Current value	417.60	466.20	524.00	2,088.96	1,854.00	260.50
13							

2. Calculate the current values by multiplying the current price by the quantity, for each of the shares

3. Select some data (e.g. the prices for USA shares) including the date column and Symbols row

	Symbol	DELL	IBM	MSFT
5	Symbol	DELL	IBM	MSFT
6	01/01/2009	38.44	108.49	43.26
7	01/01/2010	26.12	108.75	26.99
8	01/01/2011	27.49	105.28	28.16
9	01/01/2012	23.86	76.87	20.98
10	01/01/2013	33.44	98.28	24.66
11	01/01/2014	41.76	93.24	26.2

4. Click the Insert tab to view chart types then select a style from the various line types available

5. The chart appears on the current worksheet with prices for the shares plotted against the dates

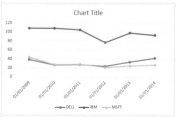

6 When the chart is selected, Chart tools of Design and Format are active, with quick links to Chart elements, Chart styles and Chart filters at the side of the chart

7 Click the Chart elements icon and select Chart Title. Choose where you want to place the chart title

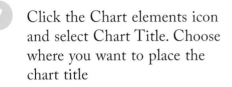

8 Click within the Chart Title box to add your text. Use the Format tab to add color and effect to the chart

9 To compare the relative values of the USA shares, select the current values. Use Ctrl and click to select non-adjacent areas such as the Symbols row

	A	B	C	D	E	F
3	Currency	us$1	us$1	us$1	£0.01	£0.01
4	Quantity	10	5	20	8	4
5	Symbol	DELL	IBM	MSFT	RR	SHEL
6	01/01/2009	38.44	108.49	43.26	175.21	391.65
7	01/01/2010	26.12	108.75	26.99	167.68	499.32
8	01/01/2011	27.49	105.28	28.16	134.24	429.92
9	01/01/2012	23.86	76.87	20.98	86.77	337.44
10	01/01/2013	33.44	98.28	24.66	175.47	347.98
11	01/01/2014	41.76	93.24	26.2	261.12	463.50
12	Current value	417.60	466.20	524.00	2,088.96	1,854.00

Current value

DELL 30%
IBM 37%
MSFT 33%

Chart1 Sheet1

10 Insert a pie chart and select a style that shows both the name and relative percentage of each. Experiment with the various styles to maximise the data being illustrated

Don't forget

Click the various parts of the chart, such as plot area and legend, to format each independently. There is more on chart formatting in the Presentations chapter (see pages 182-194).

161

Hot tip

Pre-selecting the Symbols row means that the legend appears immediately.

Don't forget

The charts can be resized, repositioned or have their own separate worksheet.

Stock on the Web

You can get stock prices and news updates on the Web, research the performance of companies, or store details of your stock portfolio, getting automatic price updates.

Hot tip

There are many other websites which provide stock information, for example you could visit the New York Stock Exchange at www.nyse.com

1. Open Internet Explorer and go to the MoneyCentral website http://money.msn.com

2. Enter the stock symbol and click Get Quote. You'll see the latest financial data for that stock item, with the current price (or the price at close, if it's outside market hours)

Hot tip

Take full advantage of the facilities offered by sites such as these. Swipe up on the screen to reveal the App bar and choose Pin to Start or Add to favorites.

3. Click the link to see Full page chart

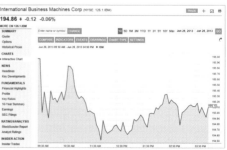

4 Open Internet Explorer and enter the website address http://finance.yahoo.com
Enter the stock symbol, or exchange symbol, and click Get Quote

Hot tip

Go to http://www. eoddata.com/symbols. aspx for a list of US stock name symbols. Use http://www. eoddata.com/stocklist/ LSE.htm for the London stockmarket.

5 When the stock summary is displayed, click the Historical Prices link

163

6 Provide Start and End dates, specify daily, weekly or monthly, and click Get Prices

7 Click Download to spreadsheet and select the option to Save. The data is downloaded to a spreadsheet on your PC and saved into the Downloads folder

Download to Spreadsheet

Hot tip

A .csv file is a comma separated variable file which can be opened in Excel.

Do you want to open or save **table.csv** from ichart.finance.yahoo.com?   Open   Save   Cancel

8 Once downloaded, the spreadsheet can be moved to another folder and edited as a normal spreadsheet

Online Banking

If you have an account at a local bank, you are probably familiar with long lines, short opening hours, high charges and low interest rates. You may have traveling time to add to the list of problems if your nearest branch has closed and you have to visit a branch in a neighboring town. The answer could be Internet banking. Online banks are available 24 hours a day and seven days a week, and you can carry out your banking transactions from home, by clicking the mouse.

Traditional Banks

Most banks and building societies offer some form of online banking. You visit the online bank using your Internet browser, and you can monitor your accounts, transfer funds, pay bills or view credit card transactions and charges. You can still use the high street branch to make deposits, or withdraw cash from the cash machine (ATM).

Virtual Banks

There are some online banks that have no branches or ATMs, and are Internet based only. This could mean lower overheads, lower charges for services and higher interest rates for balances. However, deposits must be made by mail or by transfers from another account. To withdraw cash, you'd need to use an ATM from another bank, which could mean transaction charges. Well known examples of web-only banks are NetBank and First Internet Bank.

e-Savings Accounts

Most traditional banks now have an Internet-only savings account. This is a halfway house, with the transactions being online, but with the support of a local branch.

With online accounts, you can search through your recent statements by date, amount or transaction type. You can create, amend or cancel standing orders and transfer money to another person's bank account. Making use of the faster payment systems now instigated by some banks, many payments arrive at the payee's account almost instantly.

Find Online Banks

Review the online services your current bank offers, and compare these with the services available from other banks.

To find suitable online banks and compare their accounts:

1 Visit http://www.bankrate.com/ and choose, for example, Checking and Savings

2 Select Internet-based in Find a Checking Account to view facilities, interest rates, charges and contact details for a list of banks

New Accounts
Customers opening a bank account with a bank they have not used before will usually need to provide documentation and proof of identity. The bank may need to see the paperwork, either by mail or at a local branch.

Security
Security and identity theft are the major concerns with online banking. The banks require a login ID and password. Look for the padlock symbol which indicates the site is encrypted, secure and verified as the genuine site.

Website Identification

VeriSign has identified this site as:

The Royal Bank of Scotland Group Plc
Edinburgh, Lothian
GB

This connection to the server is encrypted.

🔒 The Royal Bank of Scotla...

Online Banking Tips

When you use online banking, you must keep your sign on details safe and secure. These are some of the precautions you should take:

1. Make sure that your computer is protected from viruses and hackers by installing antivirus and firewall software, and keeping them up-to-date

2. If you receive a suspicious email message, delete it without opening it. If you get a message claiming to be from the bank that asks for your security information, ignore and delete it

3. Avoid using online banking from any public access computers such as those found in libraries, Internet cafés or universities

4. You should only access your online bank by entering the website address into your Internet browser. Do not log on to your online banking from unfamiliar websites or email links

5. Remember to verify that you are viewing the official web page. Check for the closed padlock symbol on your web browser address bar

6. Visit www.fdic.gov/ and select the Consumer Protection tab, to get advice from the Federal Deposit Insurance Corporation about protecting bank accounts and shielding yourself from identity theft and fraud. In the UK visit www.fscs.org.uk/

Don't forget

Change your password regularly, at least once a month, and avoid using common or simple words and phrases or personal details, such as birthdays.

Beware

Never disclose your online banking password details to anyone, not even someone claiming to be from the online bank.

Hot tip

With all online bank accounts, you would be advised to print off your statements regularly.

9 Digital Photography

The Built-in Cameras

Digital photography has become a major computer-related activity. The computer provides storage and editing facilities, enabling us to manage, organize and view our photographs and videos with speed and ease.

Hot tip

The cameras built in to tablets PCs do not have the high functionality and resolution of a regular camera.

Most tablet computers, such as the sample Microsoft Surface RT, have built-in cameras, one forward and one backward facing. Their function is primarily for face-to-face chatting through programs such as Skype, or for the quick, impromptu snap. The table below compares the features of the Surface RT cameras with those of the Panasonic Lumix.

Feature	Surface RT	Panasonic Lumix TZ5
Resolution	1 mp	9.1 mp
Zoom capability	None	10x optical
Wide-angle lens	No	Yes
Flash	No	Yes
Timer	Yes	Yes
Video clips	22fps	30fps
Aspect ratio	Multi	Multi

Hot tip

Although these apps are pre-installed, you are still able to visit the Store for new or updated apps.

The Surface camera in use displays a Privacy light when operating to alert potential photo subjects. The rear-facing camera is positioned to point directly forward when it is resting on its stand.

The Photography Apps

The Camera app is pre-installed on the Surface RT tablet and provides access to the basic camera functions such as changing the contrast and aspect ratio.

The Photos app, also pre-installed, manages your pictures from various sources such as the Surface itself, imported photos or from a Windows 8 phone.

Basic Operations

1 Tap or click the Camera tile to open the app. You will be informed that it needs your permission to proceed

2 Swipe to reveal the Charms bar and select Settings and then Permissions

3 Slide the bar to turn Webcam and microphone on

4 Close and re-open the app and the camera becomes available with the controls visible at the bottom of the screen

5 Tap the screen to take a photograph. The image slides away in preparation for the next shot

6 Select Change camera to switch from forward to rear facing, or vice versa. Only one camera is available at a time

7 Select Camera options to change the resolution and aspect ratio

8 Tap More for the Brightness, Contrast and Exposure controls

9 The Timer gives a three second delay after you tap the screen for a photo

Hot tip

The Camera app must be enabled before you can use the camera for snaps or video.

Don't forget

The default resolution (set when the app is installed) is usually the best option.

0.1 MP (4:3)
0.2 MP (16:9)
0.3 MP (4:3)
0.5 MP (16:9)
0.9 MP (16:9)
1.0 MP (16:10)

Video Recording

Hot tip

The Tablet PC is easier to use as a camera without the keyboard attached.

1 Tap the Video Mode button to switch from Camera mode. Similar controls are available in video mode

2 The standard default resolution is 720p (16:9). Click the down arrow to change the settings. Click More for other settings

| 240p (4:3) |
| 360p (16:9) |
| 480p (4:3) |
| 540p (16:9) |
| 720p (16:9) |
| 800p (16:10) |

3 Tap the screen to start the video recording. The timer will indicate the length of the recording. Tap again to stop recording

4 To cancel the camera function, close the Camera app in the normal way, by dragging from the top of the screen with finger or mouse

Photo Storage

Hot tip

In File Explorer view, you can select a file (photo or video) and rename it to something less obscure.

The photos you take, and the video recordings made, are automatically saved into the Camera Roll in the Photos app, which will be described later in the chapter. To view the file storage:

1 From the Start screen, choose the Desktop icon and open File Explorer. Select Libraries, the Pictures folder and Camera Roll

2 Pictures and videos are numbered sequentially, with the date, time and size indicated

Name	Date	Tags	Size	Rating
picture000	02/07/2013 23:14		203 KB	
picture001	02/07/2013 23:23		200 KB	
picture002	03/07/2013 17:06		385 KB	
picture003	03/07/2013 17:07		212 KB	
video000	02/07/2013 23:14		23,722 KB	
video001	02/07/2013 23:15		5,640 KB	
video002	02/07/2013 23:22		15,452 KB	

Connect a Camera

If you own a digital camera you can import your photos and videos to the computer to store, manage and edit them.

1. Connect your camera to a power socket, or make sure that your battery is fully charged. With the camera switched off, connect the USB cable supplied with the camera

2. When you turn the camera on, select PC mode, if applicable

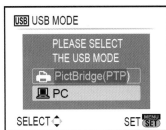

3. The computer recognizes that equipment has been attached. Tap the message to view the options available

4. First of all, note the drive letter that has been allocated to the camera – in this instance E:. You will need to know the drive letter when you detach the camera

5. To simply view the photos on your PC without importing them, use Open folder to view files

6. To copy the files onto your computer, select Import Pictures and Videos. All the photos will be displayed and selected. Tap a photo to deselect, or choose Clear selection to remove all the check marks

Beware

If the battery should fail whilst transferring photos, you could lose some data.

Don't forget

Windows does not recognize self-powered USB devices such as cameras until they are powered on. Successful connection is indicated by a sound from the PC.

Hot tip

The next time you attach the camera it should be recognized straight away, and the images presented for selection.

...cont'd

 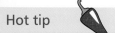
7 When you have made your selection, check the folder name, which is usually the current date. Click in the bar to change or edit the name if required, and then tap Import

8 The images are imported with a progress report and the option to open the folder when finished

9 The images are stored in the Pictures library. To further organize and edit the photos, use the Photos app which is described on page 174

10 Alternatively, use File Explorer via the Desktop tile to view and manage them

Safely Remove Hardware

It is possible to corrupt the data if you remove the camera or media at the wrong time. Follow the procedures below to safely remove hardware and Windows will apply all outstanding changes and make it safe to unplug the device:

1. Select the Desktop tile, and click the Safely Remove Hardware and Eject Media button in the Notification area at the bottom right of the Desktop

2. If the icon is hidden, click the up arrow to Show hidden icons

3. Click Customize to change the settings to have it always visible and select Show icon and notifications

4. Click the icon and then select the correct device. The disk drive letter is also shown

5. You will then get the message that it's safe to remove the hardware

Hot tip

The Safely Remove Hardware option should be used with any attached device, such as navigation systems and cameras.

Hot tip

If you turn the camera off first, you may find that the assigned drive letter is not listed. It is then safe to remove the connected equipment.

The Photos App

This app is pre-installed on all Windows 8 and Windows RT computers and is designed to create a central point of reference for all your photographic activities. It provides access to images created on the tablet itself (the Camera Roll), those on your SkyDrive, Windows phone and other devices (when connected), and Flickr and Facebook images.

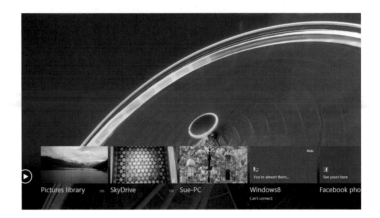

Hot tip

If you connect the camera and open the app using a different sequence, you may be asked to select the media or memory card to use.

1   Connect your camera, as described earlier, and the Photos app will open for you to transfer files

2   Follow the same procedure to select images, name the folder and import the photos

3   When finished, open the Pictures library to view the folders within. Tap any folder to open and view the contents

Choose a device to import from

If you can't see your device listed, make sure your device is turned on and connected to your PC.

Removable Disk (E:)

Secure Digital storage device (D:)

4 Swipe up on an individual image to reveal the apps bar. Editing capabilities are limited. You can:

- Run a slide show of the folder contents
- Set the image as the Lock screen image, an app tile or app background

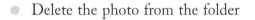

- Delete the photo from the folder
- Rotate by 90 degrees with each press
- Crop the image to remove extra details

5 To crop the image, move the frame to capture just the required area and tap Apply

6 If you are happy with the cropped image, select Save. The new image is saved as a copy, leaving the original unaltered. The cropped picture retains the same file name, appended with a (2)

7 The Photos app gives no details such as name, size, date. For that you must open the Desktop

Hot tip

Each photo is displayed for a fixed five seconds. Press the Esc key to exit the show.

Don't forget

Select the Aspect ratio icon for a list of standard dimensions or choose Custom.

175

Hot tip

Cropping the photo to a specific size is a way of applying digital zoom.

Print Your Photos

Unless you buy a dedicated photograph printer, home photo printing can be very expensive. A better option is to upload the photos to a commercial printer such as Snapfish or Kodak. However, when you do want to print, you have much greater control and function if you work in the Desktop environment.

Hot tip

You can print from the Photos app, but with limited control. With the selected image visible, swipe to reveal the Charms bar and select Devices. Then choose your printer. Select More under Devices if your printer is not initially listed.

1 Open the Desktop and File Explorer. Select the Pictures folder and the images you want to print. For more than one picture, press and hold the Shift key as you click each image

2 Right click with the mouse, or press and hold to reveal the Quick menu and select Print

Don't forget

Some of the print options depend on your particular printer. It may not, for example, be able to handle glossy paper.

3 In this window you can choose the printer, the paper size, the quality of print and paper, and the number per page. Use the scroll bar on the right to view the variety of print sizes

The Desktop environment offers much more function than the Photos app, allowing you to move, copy and re-organize your photos. You can rename them, check the size and date and edit them using the Paint program.

Photos on the Internet

1 Choose an online service, e.g. http://www.shutterfly.com/ and sign up to create an account

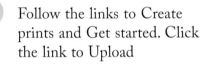

Hot tip

You could be offered your first order at a discount or a number of free prints.

2 Follow the links to Create prints and Get started. Click the link to Upload

3 Click or tap Choose files. Your Pictures folder will open for you to select the images. You may need to navigate the folders to locate the required files. Then click Open

4 The photos will be listed. Change the name for the new Album if wished and click Start to begin the upload

Hot tip

Most photographic-hosting websites offer software that you download to your computer to enable faster uploading.

NEW **EXPRESS UPLOADER**

UPLOAD PICTURES
UP TO **4X FASTER**

Get started

Additional options

- New Express Uploader
- One-by-one Uploader

- More upload options
- Upload FAQs
- See copyright policy

5 The photos can be edited online, rotated, borders added or made into photo books, cards, calendars, etc.

Alternative Photo Apps

When you visit the Windows Store, you will discover nearly 100 free photo-related apps. Each app has its particular strengths and features, but we will just look at two to highlight what they offer.

Adobe Photoshop Express

This app includes an online program, Revel, to bring together and synchronize photos across your phone, tablet and computer, or share them with friends.

Adobe Photoshop Express
★★★★☆
Free

1 Open the app and select an image to edit. Swipe up to reveal the App bar and select, for example, Red eye

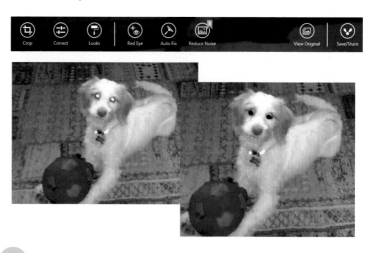

2 Follow the on screen instructions to make any changes. You can revert to the original, or save the edited photo. It will be saved with the same file name with 'edited' appended

3 Use the Edit (or selected activity such as Contrast) arrow, to return to the main menu

4 The Looks button changes the coloration, but for a wider range of effects you would need to pay for Premium looks

SuperPhoto Free

This app provides filters and effects to enhance your images and turn them into potential works of art.

1. Download and open the app. Select, for example Patterns, Mondrian, then tap Choose photo and Navigate the folders to select a suitable image

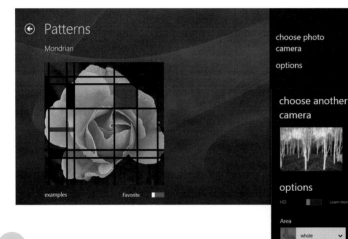

2. Click Options to choose how the effect is applied, then tap Go

3. Swipe up to reveal the App bar and select Save. Choose the location and a new file name

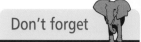

Digital Photography Tips

Hot tip

Low light conditions mean slower shutter speeds which increases the risk of camera shake.

Hot tip

The best solution is to convert your images to a lossless format such as TIFF, as soon as you download them from your camera. Edit the TIFF version, and only convert to JPEG as the last step before putting the images on the Web.

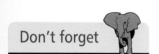

Don't forget

A *Lossless* format retains all the data from the original photo but the stored image is relatively large. A *Lossy* format sacrifices some quality to reduce the size of the stored image.

1. To minimize camera shake, use flash if possible, frame the picture through the viewfinder rather than the LCD screen, rest your elbows on a firm support, or use a tripod

2. When the viewfinder is separate from the lens, you'll see a slightly different scene. This effect, known as parallax, is negligible when you are far from your subject, but as you get closer it becomes more noticeable. So, make allowances when framing the picture through the viewfinder. Experiment at various distances, to see how the field of view in the viewfinder differs from the captured image

3. Don't panic if there are unwanted items or the wrong people encroaching on your picture. You should be able to use software to crop these from your photograph, to achieve pictures you were aiming for

4. Get as large a memory card as you can afford. Then you won't have to shuffle and delete pictures on the run, you'll be able to choose a higher quality level and take more experimental shots

5. Most digital cameras save pictures in the JPEG format. This is a lossy format, and so each time you save the picture, it loses detail and clarity. Always work on a copy of the original, and perform as many edits as possible in one session so you're not saving to the JPEG format repeatedly

6. Resize your photos before emailing them to friends, to reduce the size of the files that have to be uploaded and downloaded

10 Presentations

Create a professional presentation to support your activities or hobbies. PowerPoint has functions and styles to enhance simple slides, with transitions and effects to animate the slide show. Share your presentation in several ways, by simply printing, creating a DVD or over the Web.

PowerPoint Presentations

Slide shows created with PowerPoint can be viewed on your computer, projected with suitable equipment, posted onto the Internet, used to create a video, or saved to a CD.

182

Microsoft PowerPoint is a graphical presentation program that comes with all versions of Office. It is software that allows you to create professional-looking presentations in an easy, approachable way. Using the same ribbon-style interface present in most Office products, it provides templates, styles and functions to add interest to slide presentations.

1. Select the PowerPoint tile from the Start screen. It opens in the Desktop environment

2. The program starts with a selection of slide templates. Select Blank Presentation

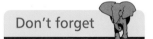

3. In the centre of the first slide are two text boxes, positioned for main title and subtitle

4. The text boxes can be repositioned or resized as required

5. Click within the box where it says Click to add title and the existing text disappears

6. Use the standard font size, style and color tools to adjust the text appearance if necessary

7. As you type, the Slides pane, to the left of the window, shows the slide content

Don't forget

Click Notes in the bottom bar to reveal the Notes area beneath the slide to add your own commentary or notes.

Add Slides

1 Click the New slide button to get the default layout on the next slide

2 Alternatively, click the down arrow underneath the New slide button to choose a different layout

3 The new slide is inserted after the current slide. The slides pane to the left provides an overview

If the design you want is not available as a template, it is easy to create your own:

1 Select the blank slide, and click the Insert tab and select Text box

2 Take the mouse to the slide and drag and draw an outline to the requisite size

3 Click inside the text box to begin typing. Use the Drawing tool enhancements, available when the cursor is inside the text box, to add color and style

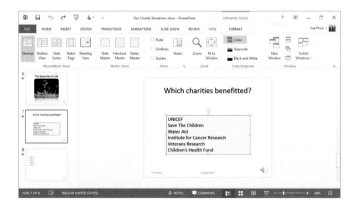

183

Using Themes

The Design tab in PowerPoint offers complete Themes to add interest and continuity to your presentation, giving it a professional finish.

1 Click the Design tab to view the Themes that are built in. Click the down arrow to display nearly 30 different slide styles

2 If you like the effect, but find the colors unsuitable, use the Variants section to select a different color palette or click the arrow next to the colors to see the full range of options

3 Fonts are included as part of the Theme and can also be modified if you wish

Insert Objects

A multitude of objects can be inserted into your presentation. PowerPoint also provides links to other Office programs to make it easy.

1 Click the Online Pictures button to add a picture from Office.com Clip Art or Bing Image Search

2 The object can be repositioned and resized. With the object selected, click the Format tab to add a frame, or effects such as shadow

3 Use Shapes to add arrows for highlighting items or SmartArt to add items such as hierarchical relationships, process diagrams and specific office-related layouts

4 All these objects can be moved, resized or edited at any time

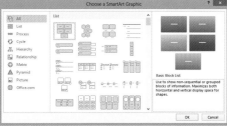

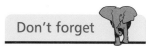

Don't forget

To resize any Clip Art object, drag the corner handle to maintain the correct proportions.

Hot tip

Shapes are just an outline object that you can type inside.

Illustrate Your Data

Microsoft Office is an integrated suite of programs, meaning that the programs work with each other. The charting function from Excel is used in PowerPoint to create graphs.

To create a chart to display data from PowerPoint:

1. On the Insert tab, click Chart

Don't forget

Select any chart style to see the preview in this window.

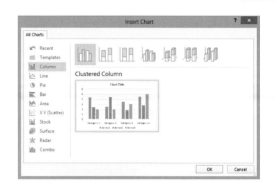

2. Select the most appropriate style and click OK. This opens a new window with a set of dummy data

Hot tip

Change the column heading to reflect the information you are displaying.

3. Edit the data and shrink or expand the selected data area as appropriate to include only your data

4. When finished, click the Close button on the spreadsheet to return to PowerPoint

5 With the chart selected, new tabs for Design and Format appear. Each part of the graph can be adjusted as necessary

6 Use the Design tab to edit or reselect the data, and also to adjust the chart style. The changes are shown as you work

7 The Format tab gives you access to tools to enhance the appearance or text such as WordArt

8 Use the Shape Styles section for further enhancements

Hot tip

If the data for your chart already exists in an Excel spreadsheet, click the Chart option in PowerPoint. When the Excel window opens, open the existing file with the data and copy and paste it into the Excel/ PowerPoint window.

187

Don't forget

On the Format tab, you can select individual areas of the chart to modify the appearance.

PowerPoint Views

PowerPoint opens in Normal view. This displays slides as the main component of the screen, with an Overview panel to the left. Select the Views tab and switch from Normal view in the Presentation View panel to Outline view, to make it easier to check the flow of the presentation.

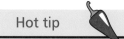

Hot tip

Several activities within PowerPoint have their own viewing and editing window.

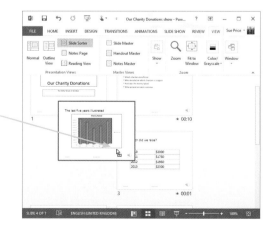

Don't forget

The slide presentation order can also be changed in the Overview panel by using the drag and drop method.

188

The Views tab gives access to the Slide sorter window, the Speaker's notes page and the Reading view. Click on each in turn to see your presentation in its most appropriate layout for the task.

Slide Sorter

Just click and drag the slides to change the order in the presentation. You will see a small box attached to the mouse arrow. The other slides reposition automatically.

Hot tip

Reading view removes the ribbon to give a full-screen layout. Press Esc on the keyboard to see the ribbon again.

Transitions

Transitions apply to the way each slide appears on the display, and there are many options.

1 Select the first slide in your presentation and click the Transitions tab. Choose any transition and you will see the effect immediately

Beware

Some Transitions are rather vibrant and should be used sparingly!

2 Click the down arrow to the right of the Transition selection pane to see the full list of options, categorized as Subtle, Exciting or Dynamic

3 When you have chosen the transition, click the Effects Option button to have yet more choice on how the transition appears

Hot tip

The Effects Option changes to reflect the transition chosen.

4 The chosen transition applies only to the selected slide. Click the Apply to All box to have consistency throughout the presentation

5 Other settings on the Transitions tab let you add sounds, change the duration and how to advance to the next slide. Advance on mouse click is the default. Use the After number of seconds timing to advance for a self-running presentation

Animations

Animations are applied to the individual parts of each slide. So, for example, the bulleted list slide illustrated here, has several parts:

Hot tip

The Preview button shows the animations in action. Press Shift + F5 to run the slide show from the selected slide.

Hot tip
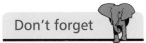

Bullet points can be individually selected and different animations applied to each.

Don't forget

Use the Animation Painter to copy animations from one slide to another.

1. Click the Animations tab and title of the slide. Select an animation such as Fly In and the effect is immediately demonstrated

2. For the bulleted list, click inside the text box and apply an animation

3. Click or tap the Animations pane option to show the pane on the right, allowing you to modify each item, to change the order in which they appear or to remove the animation

4. Click Effect Options for further refinements. Note that each line will appear individually By Paragraph

5. The slide show is usually advanced by pressing the spacebar or by mouse click. This applies to slides or for each animation within the slide

Run the Slide Show

Click the Slide Show tab and the button From beginning to view the whole presentation, remembering to press the spacebar or click the mouse to progress if required.

The Slide Show tab offers very many options to fine tune the show to make it suitable for different audiences:

- Custom Slide Show allows you to choose specific slide combinations from the full presentation, name and save the subset as a separate slide show

- Set Up Slide Show includes choices for where it will be shown, such as a kiosk or full screen. It includes options to loop continuously and for the laser pointer

- Change the resolution to the most appropriate for the medium being used. The resolution can affect the speed or the clarity of the show. Many projectors have a maximum resolution of 1024 by 768 pixels

Use Presenter View

- Use Presenter View. This lets you use two monitors, one full-screen and one with the Speaker notes and timings

Rehearse Timings, Record Slide Show
Run the slide show with Rehearse Timings and a small timing box appears on the screen. It records the length of time each slide is shown. When finished, it presents the slides with individual timings indicated.

Click the option to Record Slide Show. The recording is saved with the file. You can clear Timings or Animations or simply re-record the show if you wish to make adjustments.

Hot tip

Press F5 at any time to view the slide show in its entirety.

Hot tip

To show a laser pointer during the show, hold down the Ctrl key and press the left mouse button.

191

Don't forget

With a microphone attached to your computer you can add narration. This would be particularly useful if the show is to run unattended.

Print Options

1 Click the File tab and Print to view printing options

2 To print only the slides is straightforward – just click Print. You can also specify individual slides or ranges, for example 1,3,4 or 5-8

3 Click Full Page Slides to select what and how you wish to print

4 Notes Pages prints a copy of one slide per page, with your speaker's notes below

5 Outline prints a text only version of each slide, as seen in Outline view on the main slide screen

6 Handouts is obviously the most economical way to print the slides selecting how many per page

7 Click the Color button if you prefer to print in greyscale or black and white

8 A Header and Footer can be added to the slides, either here or in the main slide view by selecting the Insert tab

Publication Issues

PowerPoint presentations are usually designed for general viewing to family, clubs, small business, as promotional material, for charity activities, etc. As creator of the slide show, you may wish to keep a degree of control over whether the presentation can be altered, by whom and by how much.

 Click the File tab and the Info option

2 The default setting is to allow anyone to open, copy or change any part of the presentation

3 Click Protect Presentation to see to what degree you can protect your production, and if required, select appropriately

Prepare for Sharing

1 Click Check for Issues and Inspect Document. View the list that it will inspect and click Inspect

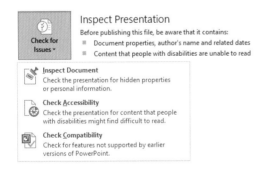

2 Items that cause concern will be noted with the option to Remove All

Hot tip

All programs within Microsoft Office contain details, such as the name of the creator, of those who have edited the file, the time spent editing, etc. In most situations this is not a problem. With a PowerPoint presentation there may be times when you wish to withhold some of this information from public view.

Save and Share

PowerPoint offers many ways to save your slide show and to share it with others.

1   Click the File tab and select Share to view the options. Invite People uses your SkyDrive account

2   Present Online again uses the Internet and a Microsoft account

3   Publish Slides stores slides in a shared location with the possibility of shared editing

Don't forget

You will need to decide what level of protection you require to put in place (see previous page).

Hot tip

SharePoint can be a home server or web-based. Its purpose is to share files, contacts and calendars.

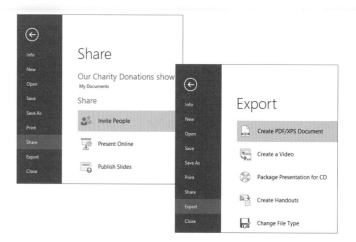

Export

- Create a Video incorporates the transmissions, animations and narration, and can be saved to disk or the Web

- Package Presentation for CD creates a CD that can be run on most computers

- Create Handouts in Word format that are automatically updated when the slides change

- Choose Change File Type to save as an older version of PowerPoint, a template, a picture show, etc.

11 Personalize Windows

In this chapter you will see how to change settings to make your computer the way you want it. Reposition, add and resize tiles, use your own photos as the Desktop background and adjust the screen and mouse to suit your own requirements.

Screen Backgrounds

When Windows 8 opens for the first time you are offered a choice of background colors for the Start screen. To change this setting at any point:

1 Bring up the Charms bar and select Settings. Start to type and select Start screen from the Search field

2 Select a new background color from the color bar and at the same time experiment with the background images that are offered

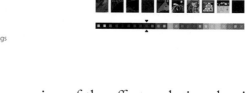

3 You get a preview of the effect each time, but its a good idea to check the actual effect when you are back at the Start screen

The Desktop Background

The Desktop environment offers a wider choice of options.

1. Swipe to reveal the Charms bar, select Settings as before and start to type "desktop"

2. Select the entry Change desktop background

3. The standard is the Windows daisy, but you can choose from other flowers or the Earth category

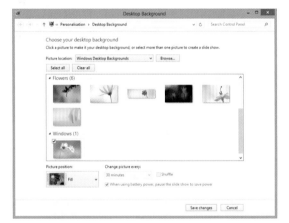

These images are from Windows Desktop Backgrounds, but you have the ability to use your own pictures, or a plain background if preferred.

4. Click the arrow to view the folder list or Browse to find the required image

5. If you Select all (pictures) they will change every 30 minutes or your chosen frequency, creating a form of slide show

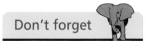

Don't forget

When you change the image on the Desktop, it changes the image on the Desktop tile.

Hot tip

If using a laptop or Tablet PC, make sure to tick the box to save battery power.

Hot tip

You will need to save any changes made to the Desktop background settings.

197

Your Account Image

Select your username in the top corner and tap Change account picture to open the PC settings and Personalize option

Sue
Price

Change account picture

Lock

Sign out

PC settings

Lock screen   Start screen   Account picture

Personalise

Users

Notifications

Search

Share

General

Privacy

Devices

Wireless

Ease of Access

Sync your settings

HomeGroup

Browse

Create an account picture

Camera

People

1 Tap Camera to take a picture of yourself using the camera built in to the Tablet. To take the snap, just tap the screen. You then have the option to move or resize the focus, or to try again

OK   Retake

2 Alternatively, choose Browse to use an existing photo. If the required photo is not displayed, use Go up to locate another folder, select the folder to open it, and then the image

Files ⌄ Pictures
Go up   Sort by name ⌄

Rotary Weekend

Screenshots

Choose image   Cancel

Files ⌄ Rotary Weekend
Go up   Sort by name ⌄

Choose image   Cancel

Organize the Start Screen

The selection of tiles displayed on the Windows 8 Start screen can vary with the supplier. You may also have downloaded other apps, like those suggested in Chapter 3. Tiles can be organized to suit your preference.

 Select a tile, either with the right mouse button, or with touch (hold and drag down slightly)

2 From the App Bar, you can choose: Unpin from Start, Uninstall, Smaller (or larger) or Turn live tile off (or on)

3 Live tiles for News, Finance, Trending and Travel, can be a distraction. Their purpose is to bring you the latest information without the necessity of searching for it. Select them individually to turn them off

4 Select and hold a tile to drag it to a new position. The other tiles will automatically reflow into position. This also occurs when you resize or unpin tiles

New tiles appear automatically when you download an app. To reinstate one that has been removed:

1 Swipe to reveal the Apps bar and select All apps. Choose the app (as in no. 1 above) and tap Pin to Start

2 The tile appears to the right of the existing tiles

Hot tip

You can't just click or touch the tile as that runs the program.

Don't forget

Uninstall will completely remove the program from the computer.

Hot tip

The Photos app is also a live tile that can be disabled.

Group Tiles

Start screen tiles can be arranged in groups to bring together sets of related apps such as entertainment or reading. To create a group:

 Select a tile and start to drag it across the screen from its current position

2 As you drag the tile, a bar appears to show you when to drop the tile to create or join a group. Release the tile when you see it

Hot tip

The Zoom out button only appears when you have a mouse attached and use the scroll bar at the bottom of the screen.

3 Repeat with each tile to make the group

4 Pinch or zoom out to view the group in its location

Hot tip

Only when you have zoomed out, are you able to name or move the group.

5 Drag down or right-click to select the group of tiles, and then select the option to Name group

6 Tap or click anywhere to restore the tiles to their regular size

Customize the Desktop

As seen previously in this chapter, the Desktop provides a very different approach and working environment. The Microsoft Office programs operate on the Desktop, even though they have tiles on the Start screen.

On the Surface Tablet PC, a version of Microsoft Office is already installed, with both tiles on the Start screen and icons on the Taskbar on the Desktop.

On a different tablet or computer, you may have installed Microsoft Office yourself. The Office program tiles will be added automatically to the Start screen, but it's very convenient to also have them as shortcuts on the Desktop. To add the shortcut icon:

1. From the Start screen, swipe or right-click to reveal the Apps bar and select All apps

2. Click or drag down to select the individual program, then select Pin to Taskbar

3. In the Desktop environment you can have several programs open at once. You can use the Taskbar icons to open or switch between the programs

201

Don't forget
Any program that works in the Desktop environment can have a shortcut added to the Taskbar.

Hot tip
Use the option Pin to Start for programs such as Calculator, that you use frequently.

Add Desktop Shortcuts

For frequently-used programs or files, it is useful to add a shortcut icon directly onto the desktop.

Hot tip

The shortcut can be to a folder or an individual file, as well as a program.

1   Select the Desktop tile and open File Explorer and My Documents to locate a frequently-used document

Hot tip

The arrow on the new icon indicates that it is a Shortcut to the file or program

2   Using a mouse, right-click and drag the document to the Desktop. When you release the mouse button, select Create Shortcuts here as the best action

| Copy here |
| **Move here** |
| Create shortcuts here |
| Cancel |

3   Without a mouse attached, you can only drag the file which then moves the file to the desktop

Organize the Desktop Shortcuts

With a number of shortcuts on the Desktop:

Don't forget

Deleting the shortcut on the desktop will not delete the application.

1   Right-click the Desktop (using the mouse or the keypad) or press and hold the screen to open the menu. Select from any of the options to manage and arrange the Desktop shortcuts

View	▶		Large icons
Sort by	▶	•	Medium icons
Refresh			Small icons
Paste			Auto arrange icons
Paste shortcut		✔	Align icons to grid
Undo Move	Ctrl+Z	✔	Show desktop icons
New	▶		
Screen resolution			
Personalise			

Mouse Buttons

Even with the new Touch controls in Windows 8, an attached mouse can make life easier, especially with Office programs and in the Desktop environment. To manage the mouse settings:

1 Swipe to reveal the Charms bar, select Settings and type Mouse into the Search field

2 Select Mouse and if you are left-handed, click the Button configuration box to switch primary and secondary mouse buttons

3 Use the folder icon to test the double-click setting. If the folder doesn't open or close, click and drag the slider to a slower setting

4 Click OK when you are happy with the response for the action

Hot tip

Although the Search reveals nearly 20 results, most of them direct you to the same Mouse Properties dialog box to make the changes.

203

Don't forget

If you switch the mouse buttons, you would then press the Right button to select items, and the Left button to display action menus – the reverse of the usual procedures.

Pointer Options

If you find yourself losing track of the location of the mouse pointer, there are several options that can help.

 Display the Mouse Properties and click the Pointer Options tab

 Move the slider to adjust the relative speed of the pointer

Mouse Properties

| Buttons | Pointers | Pointer Options | Wheel | Hardware |

Motion
Select a pointer speed:
Slow ——— Fast
☑ Enhance pointer precision

Snap To
☐ Automatically move pointer to the default button in a dialogue box

Visibility
☐ Display pointer trails
Short ——— Long
☑ Hide pointer while typing
☐ Show location of pointer when I press the CTRL key

OK   Cancel   Apply

3️⃣ Select Snap To, to have the pointer move to the most likely choice, the OK button for example, when you open a new window

4️⃣ Locate the pointer easily by choosing to display a pointer trail, or by setting the Ctrl key to highlight the current pointer position

5️⃣ To adjust your mouse wheel, open Mouse Properties, select the Wheel tab and specify that each click scrolls a screenful of information, or a specified number of lines. The default is to move 3 lines

Display Management

To view the options for your display:

1 Right-click or press and hold anywhere on the Desktop for the menu and select Screen Resolution

2 The example illustrated below is of a Surface PC with the current monitor displayed (1). If a second monitor was attached it would be indicated

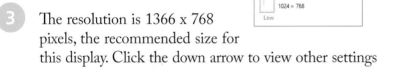

3 The resolution is 1366 x 768 pixels, the recommended size for this display. Click the down arrow to view other settings

4 If you have problems reading text and other items, click the line Make text and other items larger or smaller

5 Try Medium 125% or Larger 150% if offered. You will be prompted to close all programs and Log in again to see the effect

Hot tip

If you have a notebook, laptop or Tablet PC with a small screen, you can attach a larger monitor.

Don't forget

You can lower the resolution. This will make the text and icons on the screen appear larger. However, other methods such as Magnifier, Zoom or the method described here do this more effectively.

Hot tip

Changes to the resolution or text only affect the Desktop environment.

Ease of Access Center

Hot tip

Make sure to use the Ease of Access Center, rather than just Ease of Access. The Center offers the full range of options to help you customize your system to meet your vision, hearing, or mobility requirements.

Hot tip

The problems and solutions relate to sight, dexterity, hearing, speech and reasoning (concentration).

Don't forget

If you do change your mind, you can revisit the Ease of Access Center and make a different set of choices.

1. Search Settings on the Start Screen and type Ease of Access Center

2. The Narrator voice will start automatically and step through the options available

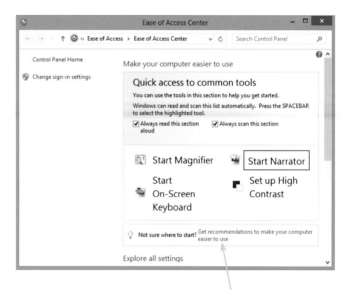

3. If you want advice, click Get recommendations to make your computer easier to use

4. The on-screen prompts take you through a series of questions to help identify problems you may have

5. When you have finished, the Ease of Access Center will recommend options to help to make your computer easier to use

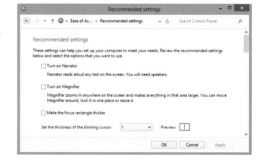

Accessibility Tools

Narrator
This is a text-to-speech program that helps users who are blind or partially sighted. It reads aloud the content of screens, windows and typed information.

Narrator is designed to work with Notepad, Control Panel programs, Internet Explorer, the Windows desktop, and Windows setup. Narrator may not read words aloud correctly in other programs.

Magnifier
Use this tool to magnify anywhere on the screen. Magnifier starts with the magnification level at 200% and all items on the screen, including the Tiles, are immediately twice as big.

1. Move the mouse pointer to the item on which you want to focus

2. To change settings or close Magnifier, move the mouse onto the small magnifying glass and click

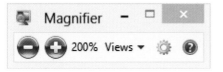

Sticky Keys
The Sticky keys feature allows you to work one-handed. Key combinations involving modifier keys (Ctrl, Alt, Shift or Windows Logo key) are selected one key at a time. To activate Sticky keys press the Shift key five times in succession. To disable it, go to the Ease of Access Center.

Don't forget

Other text-to-speech programs are readily available and can significantly enhance access to the computer.

Beware

When you start Magnifier, the display becomes twice as big. Scroll bars do not appear, so you need to move the mouse to the edges of the screen to view objects currently hidden.

Hot tip

If one of the supported key combinations is used normally, two keys pressed at once, Sticky keys is turned off.

PC Settings

① Swipe from the right or use the Hotspot on the right to reveal the Charms bar and select Settings, Change PC settings

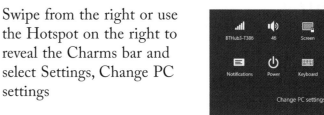

② Within this list you can view and change a variety of factors that affect the way your computer works

Personalize
This initially shows the Lock screen. Within Personalize you can:

- Browse to select a different image for the Lock screen

- Choose apps to run in the background, or display updated status, for example Calendar. If an item is added to the Calendar for the current date, it will show on the Lock screen

- Change the Start screen and the Account picture (these topics were covered earlier in the chapter)

Users

Within Users you can:

- Access your online account

- Change your password

- Create a picture password

- Create, (or Change or Remove a PIN once created) for the computer

Your account

Sue Price
sue.j.price@live.com

You can switch to a local account, but your settings won't sync between the PCs you use.

Switch to a local account

More account settings online

Sign-in options

Change your password

Create a picture password

Create a PIN

Require a password after the display has been off for

15 minutes

The PIN password is an easier alternative to your original sign-in to the computer. You must still use your original sign-in to access your account.

General

This category allows you to set options such as:

- Date and time

- Delete history. Select this to close all open apps in one action. Unusually, there is no warning, you are just informed 'Done!'

- Change the way the keyboard works when typing. This includes Autocorrect and highlighting misspelled words

- Change language preferences. This allows you to change the keyboard layout to accommodate foreign characters

- See how much space your apps take in case you need more storage room

Time

12:38, 06 May 2013

(UTC) Dublin, Edinburgh, Lisbon, London

Adjust for daylight saving time automatically
On

App switching

Allow switching between recent apps
On

When I swipe in from the left edge, switch to my most recent app
On

Delete history

Touch keyboard

Show text suggestions as I type
On

Add a space after I choose a text suggestion
On

App sizes

Music		144 MB
Microsoft Solitaire Collection		140 MB
Games		105 MB
Photos		105 MB
Mail, Calendar, People and Messaging		98.0 MB
Video		65.4 MB

Hot tip

The picture password uses one of your photos. Follow the prompts to select the image. You then use three gestures, a combination of circles, straight lines and taps to draw directly on the screen. The size, position and direction become part of the password.

209

Synchronize Your Settings

Having changed settings to suit your requirements, you can take advantage of the Sync your settings feature in the PC settings menu.

Hot tip

With more than one computer using Windows 8, Sync your settings can make switching between devices much easier.

Hot tip

When roaming, metered connections can be very expensive, particularly in a foreign country. For this reason, this option is turned off.

1 Open PC setting and select Sync your settings

2 The first and over-riding option is to Sync settings on this PC. If you turn this off, all other settings become unavailable

3 Of particular value is the ability to sync Passwords, Ease of Access and Language preferences

Sync your settings

Sync settings on this PC
On

Settings to sync

Personalise
Colours, background, lock screen and your account picture
On

Desktop personalisation
Themes, taskbar, high contrast and more
On

Passwords
Sign-in info for some apps, websites, networks and HomeGroup
On

Ease of Access
High contrast, Narrator, Magnifier and more
On

Language preferences
Keyboards, other input methods, display language and more
On

App settings
Certain settings in your apps
On

4 Sync your settings over metered connections is on by default, as you will normally be operating from within home boundaries

Sync over metered connections

Sync settings over metered connections
On

Sync settings over metered connections even when I'm roaming
Off

5 If you sign on with your Microsoft account on a public or shared machine, your personal settings will be downloaded, so you may prefer to use a Guest account (see page 216)

12 Manage Your Computer

You can share your PC with other family members, or with guests, without having to worry about your settings getting changed or your data being overwritten. Set up or join a HomeGroup to share your music, photos and printers, and make sure your computer is secure and up-to-date.

Sharing Your PC

If you let others use your PC, you'll soon find that your settings get changed and favorites get amended, and you'll have to spend time putting things back the way they were. Other people's files will be mixed in with yours, and you could lose information if they accidentally modify your files, or save a file using one of your file names. To solve this, Windows 8 allows each user to have a separate account, with individual settings and preferences. Users log on with their own usernames, and see only the settings and the data that belongs to them.

There are three types of user accounts, but these may not all be present on your system:

- Administrator (provides the most control)
- Standard (for everyday computing use)
- Guest (for temporary use by visitors)

To see all the accounts defined on your system:

1 From the Start screen, swipe up to show the Charms bar and type Control Panel into the Search field

2 In Control Panel, select User Accounts and Family Safety, then Add or remove user accounts

3 This has two accounts, one defined as Administrator, and one Standard. The guest account is switched off

Create an Account

You must be signed on with a username that has the computer administrator authority to be able to add other users.

1 Swipe to reveal the Charms bar and select Settings, then Change PC settings

2 On the Users option, swipe or scroll to Add a user

Hot tip

You should give Standard accounts to inexperienced users. You could even change your personal account to Standard once you've set it up. This reduces the risk of hackers misusing your system. However, you must always have an Administrator account available to maintain your system.

213

3 You are asked to provide a Microsoft account email address for the new account user, and given the opportunity to sign up for one if necessary

Hot tip

Signing in with a Microsoft account means that your new user will have access to their online Microsoft documents and also their specific PC settings.

...cont'd

Hot tip

You can supply any email address, but you will need to create a Microsoft account, if the email address is not already associated with one.

④ Click Next and you will be told that you should advise the new account holder that they will need to sign in the first time they use the account

⑤ Tick the box to turn on Family Safety if it's a child's account. Then click or tap Finish

⑥ The new account will be listed in Users in PC Settings

Local Account
Follow the steps above but sign up for a local account. For a child in particular, this is a useful option. They are unlikely to have documents online that they want to access, and personalized PC settings that they want available from another computer. It also takes away the ability to download apps from the Windows Store.

You will need to supply just a name and password to be used at the Lock screen at start up.

Manage User Accounts

① You will need to sign on to the computer with your Administrator account

② Swipe to reveal the Charms bar and select Settings. Type User into the Search field and select User Accounts from the results

Hot tip

You must open the individual Users account to add an account image. See page 217.

③ Select Manage my account and you are switched to PC settings where your own details can be changed

④ Select Manage another account and then the account itself. The options are:

● Set up Family Safety (see page 107)
● Change account type from Standard to Administrator
● Delete the account

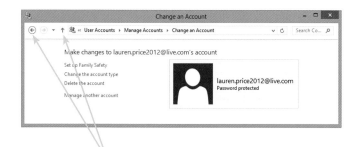

⑤ Use the arrows to navigate backwards to a previous window, or up to return to the higher level of the Control Panel

The Guest Account

The Windows Guest account allows someone who isn't a regular user of your computer to operate it with limited access. No password is required, and visitors can browse the Internet, or write and print documents and so on. Guest users do not have access to password-protected files, folders or system settings.

The Guest account is normally turned off. To turn it on:

1. From the Start screen, swipe to reveal the Charms bar, select Settings and type Guest account into the Search field

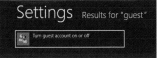

2. Tap or click the result which opens the Manage Accounts window on the Desktop. Select the Guest account

3. Click the button to Turn On the Guest Account. This will add it to the Sign-in screen

4. The Guest account gives your visitor access to the Office programs, if installed, to Internet Explorer, the Desktop and the Windows Store

5. If they go to the Windows Store they will need to supply Microsoft account details before they are able to purchase free or paid for apps

Switch User

With two or more users registered on the computer, you can allow another to sign on whilst you are still logged on.

1 From the Start screen, tap or click the username or account picture

2 Click or tap the Lock option if you wish to stay logged in but are leaving the computer for a time

3 Select Sign out if you are completely finished. Any apps that were open in your working session will be closed, but web pages visited will be remembered when you next open Internet Explorer

4 Select a different user account and you are immediately transferred to their Sign-in screen

5 If you have selected the wrong account, click the Back arrow to return to the main Sign-in screen which shows all users accounts

Don't forget

The first time the new user opens the account, Windows 8 will prepare appropriate settings. Users with a Microsoft account will have their settings synchronized. While this is happening, Windows offers a short tutorial.

Hot tip

The Guest account does not have a sign-in password

Beware

If you shut down the computer completely, you will be warned if other users are signed in and that they could lose any unsaved work. In this case you should sign out instead.

HomeGroup

Your Tablet computer or new Windows 8 device may not be your only computer. You may also have a laptop to travel with, or a desktop for a better screen. You could have music files or an all-in-one printer that you would like to access from either machine. All of these scenarios suggest the creation of a home network.

1. Open PC Settings from the Charms bar and select Change PC Settings

2. Choose HomeGroup to display the current status

> **PC settings**
>
> Sync your settings
>
> HomeGroup
>
> Windows Update
>
> **HomeGroup**
>
> **Create a homegroup**
> With a homegroup you can share libraries and devices with other people on this network. You can also stream media to devices.
>
> Your homegroup is protected with a password, and you'll always be able to choose what you share.
>
> Create

3. Click Create for the HomeGroup to be created. A password is set and shareable resources are listed

> **PC settings**
>
> Personalize
>
> Users
>
> Notifications
>
> Search
>
> Share
>
> General
>
> Privacy
>
> Devices
>
> Ease of Access
>
> Sync your settings
>
> HomeGroup
>
> Windows Update
>
> Libraries and devices
> When you share content, other homegroup members can see it, but only you can change it.
>
> Documents
> Not shared
>
> Music
> Not shared
>
> Pictures
> Not shared
>
> Videos
> Not shared
>
> Printers and devices
> Not shared
>
> Media devices
> Allow all devices on the network such as TVs and game consoles to play my shared content
>
> Off
>
> Membership
> If someone else wants to join your homegroup, give them this password:
>
> wC28q7ve6u
>
> If you leave the homegroup, you won't be able to get to shared libraries or devices.
>
> Leave

4. Decide which resources you wish to share and tap or click those switches, for example Music, Pictures and Videos

5. Sharing Media Devices will allow games consoles and Internet-connected TVs to gain access to the shared items

Join the HomeGroup

1. Open the Charms bar, select Change PC Settings and then HomeGroup

2. You will need to enter the HomeGroup password that was created when setting up the new HomeGroup

3. The password is a combination of numbers and letters, randomly generated, but can be changed later if you wish to have something more memorable

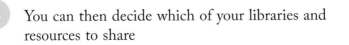

4. You can then decide which of your libraries and resources to share

Windows RT HomeGroup

Windows RT on the Surface Tablet is more limited in its HomeGroup capacity than the full Windows 8 operating system. You cannot create your own HomeGroup and you cannot make your own libraries available to others, but you do have access to theirs.

Don't forget

You are advised that you can only access others' libraries and devices, but not share your own.

1 Open PC Settings and HomeGroup to see if a HomeGroup exists. Type the required password and tap Join

2 To view the HomeGroup and explore shared libraries and devices, open File Explorer on the Desktop

3 Select HomeGroup to expand the entry and see which members are on the network. Select a specific PC to view which folders are shared

Action Center

The Action Center monitors your system for security and maintenance issues, and generates alerts if it encounters a problem. The Action Center runs in the background whilst your PC is switched on. To open the Action Center:

1 Reveal the Charms bar, select Settings and type Action Center into the Search field

2 Alternatively, click the flag in the Notification area on the Desktop. You will see a list of any outstanding issues and can open the Action Center from the link provided

Hot tip

If you choose to archive the message, you can view it later by selecting the link in the Action Center.

221

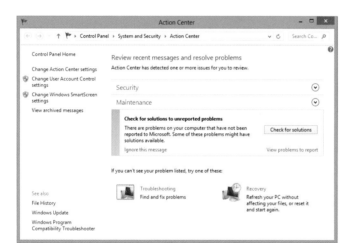

3 Select the button, Check for solutions, and then if appropriate Send information

Don't forget

When a solution to any of the problems becomes available, a message will be sent to the Action Center.

...cont'd

Security

1 Click the down arrow on Security to expand the list of security settings

Hot tip

Click Change Action Center settings to adjust your current security settings.

Click Windows Update to see any updates waiting to be applied.

- Windows Firewall should be On
- Windows Update should be On
- Virus Protection is On
- Spyware/unwanted software protection should be On
- Internet security settings should be OK
- Windows SmartScreen should be On
- User Account Control should be On
- Network Access Protection relates to corporate environments only

Uninstall an App

As you work with your PC, surf the Internet and visit the Windows Store, you will probably download many programs that seem like a good idea at the time, but are seldom used or you find unsuitable. To uninstall a program:

 From the Start screen, swipe up to select the All apps button and locate the redundant app

Hot tip

When you install a program, entries get added to the Start screen, to the registry and you may have a shortcut added to your desktop. Uninstalling the program removes all these entries and should remove the software properly.

223

Right mouse click or press and hold the app to select it, then select Uninstall on the app bar

Uninstall a Program

 Search Settings in the Charms bar for Uninstall a program. Tap the result to open the Control Panel, Programs and Features window

Hot tip

There are no programs on the Surface RT that can be uninstalled.

Select Uninstall or Change to add or remove features

Windows Update

Updates are changes or additions that will help to fix problems or improve the performance of the computer. They are for Windows but you can enable Microsoft Update for other products such as Office. To view the Update status:

To check what updates are available for your Windows system, you'll need an active Internet connection.

1 From the Start screen, swipe to reveal the Charms bar and select Search. Tap Settings and type Update in the Search field

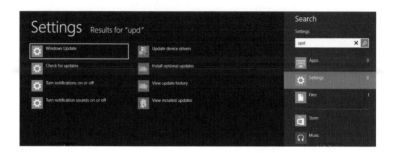

Don't forget

Updates are usually applied at shut down, so you'll be warned to leave the computer running.

2 Click the entry in the results list. Windows Update will inform you of updates available for your system

3 Click Install updates to apply the available updates. Your computer will need to restart after installing any updates. Save your work and ensure that your battery is charged before you begin

Hot tip

With the full version of Windows 8, you can choose to turn Automatic Updates on or off. With Windows RT, there is no option to turn off automatic updates.

PC settings

| Users |
| Notifications |
| Search |
| Share |
| General |
| Privacy |
| Devices |
| Wireless |
| Ease of Access |
| Sync your settings |
| HomeGroup |
| Windows Update |

Windows Update

A firmware update is available for your PC

We will restart your PC to install this update. Take a moment to save your work and make sure that your PC's battery is charged before you continue.

3 updates will be installed

Install and Restart

4 You can also check for Updates manually. From the same Search results as shown on the previous page, click Check for updates

With Windows 8 and RT you may be informed that the system will install updates in a few days' time. This early warning is because normally the computer goes to sleep or will hibernate rather than completely shut down.

PC settings

Users
Notifications
Search
Share
General
Privacy
Devices
Wireless
Ease of Access
Sync your settings
HomeGroup
Windows Update

Windows Update

You're set to automatically install updates

No important updates are scheduled to be installed. We last checked today. We'll continue to check for newer updates daily.

There are some other updates available. Get more information

225

5 Select the text 'No important updates are scheduled...' and then 'Get more information' to open Windows Update in the Control Panel

6 Use this window to View your update History and to see Installed updates

You should only uninstall an Update if advised by a technician, or if the computer fails immediately after a particular Update.

Mobility Center

The Mobility Center is a collection of settings used with a laptop computer to help with power and connections.

 Type Mobility Center into the Search field on the Charms bar and tap Settings. Click the program link

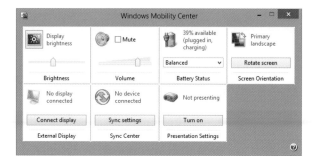

Click an icon, such as Display brightness, to open the options panel and change the settings

For Presentations click the icon to view settings available. Your computer stays awake, and you can select background image and volume

Battery and power management is handled using the icon in the Notification area on the Desktop. Click the battery symbol and select More power options

File History

File History, new to Windows 8, will automatically keep a copy of your files in the Libraries, Desktop, Favorites and Contacts folders. It uses an external drive to take a regular copy of your work. To turn on File History:

 Reveal the Charms bar, select Settings and type File History into the Search field. Tap File History in the Results to open the window with details

 File History will search for a suitable drive and offer the option to Turn on

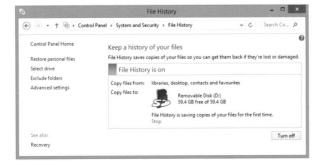

Immediately, copies are taken of your files and regular backups created

Hot tip

File History replaces the Backup program included in previous versions of Windows. It is designed to make it easier to protect your files and get back copies when things go wrong. Once turned on, it runs discreetly in the background.

227

Hot tip

Use the option to Select drive if you are connected to a network or have an alternative removable drive.

Available drives
Removable Disk (D:)
INTENSO (E:)
\\Premium-pc\c\SurfaceBackup

...cont'd

Hot tip

If any information on your hard disk is accidentally erased, overwritten or becomes inaccessible because of a hard disk malfunction, you'll quickly learn why it is important to make backup copies – before such problems arise.

Hot tip

Select any file in File Explorer and click History on the Menu bar. It will display previous versions of the file.

File History copies are created hourly and will be kept until the available space has been used, when older copies will be overwritten. To view the settings:

1. Click or tap Advanced settings. You can change the regularity of copies, amount of disk space used and how long copies are kept

2. Choose Restore personal files to open and browse the copies stored

3. The blue arrows take you forward and backwards in time. Click the green arrow in the middle to restore the file. You will be guided through the process of restoring the file to your chosen location

System Restore

You may wish to restore system files, for example if you've experienced system problems after installing new hardware or software. You can use the System Restore feature for this.

1 Search for Recovery in Settings on the Charms bar

2 Click Open System Restore. Using System Restore does not affect your items such as your documents, pictures or music, it mainly affects system changes

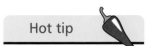

Hot tip

System Restore is not offered in Windows RT, see page 231 for alternatives.

229

3 Select a date and time that is before the problem occurred, clicking Show more restore points if necessary

Don't forget

Windows will automatically recommend the most recent restore point, but you may wish to use an older one.

4 Tap or click Next and, finally, click Finish to accept your chosen date and time (see page 230)

...cont'd

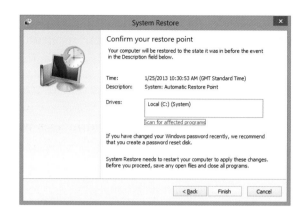

Don't forget

System Restore cannot be interrupted, but it can be undone.

⑤ You will need to confirm once more that this is the required action. Click or tap Yes

⑥ You will be advised when the Restore point has been successfully applied

⑦ The computer will need to restart to apply the changes. If the selected restore point does not fix the problem, undo the restore point and try another one

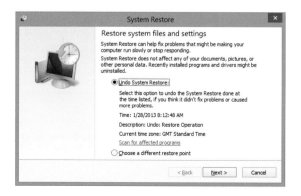

Recovery Features

Windows 8 and RT offer other ways of resetting your system when things aren't working as they should. In the General section of PC settings you can:

- Refresh the computer but leave your work, music, photo and video files untouched. Any personalization such as your account photo and background images will remain, as well as downloaded apps. Your PC settings will be restored to its defaults.

- Remove all the contents and reset to factory settings. Your personal files, photos, etc. will be removed and any apps you have installed. All settings will be restored to their defaults.

- Start your computer from an external source such as an attached USB drive or DVD. This option would be used if you needed to change your firmware settings or Windows start-up settings. Your PC would be restarted.

Hot tip

Even though you restore to factory settings and any apps are removed, Windows Store will remember those you have purchased and allow you to download them again.

231

PC settings

Personalise	Language preferences
Users	**Available storage**
Notifications	You have 41.1 GB available. See how much space your apps are using.
Search	**View app sizes**
Share	
General	**Refresh your PC without affecting your files**
Privacy	If your PC isn't running well, you can refresh it without losing your photos, music, videos and other personal files.
Devices	**Get started**
Wireless	
Ease of Access	**Remove everything and reinstall Windows**
Sync your settings	If you want to recycle your PC or completely start again, you can reset it to its factory settings.
HomeGroup	**Get started**

Advanced start-up

Start up from a device or disc (such as a USB drive or DVD), change your PC's firmware settings, or change Windows start-up settings. This will restart your PC.

Restart now

- You can create a recovery drive to reset your PC or troubleshoot problems in the Recovery window in the Control Panel, as described on page 229.

Recovery

Control Panel ▸ All Control Panel Items ▸ Recovery   Search Co...

Control Panel Home

Advanced recovery tools

Create a recovery drive
Create a recovery drive to refresh or reset your PC, or to troubleshoot problems, even when it can't start.

See also
File History

System Properties

To see details of your computer's processor, memory and operating system:

1 Type system into the Search field and select Settings. Select System from the results

2 Click Windows Experience Index to see details of your computer's performance rating

3 You can identify the weak points in your system and improve performance by, for example, changing the hard disk or adding memory or upgrading the graphics card

Index

233

N

O

P